A NEW HUMANISM

*The University Addresses of
Daisaku Ikeda*

New York • WEATHERHILL • *Tokyo*

First Edition, 1996

Published by Weatherhill, Inc., of New York and Tokyo, with editorial offices at 568 Broadway, Suite 705, New York, NY, 10012.

Library of Congress Cataloging-in-Publication Data:
Ikeda, Daisaku.
[Speeches. English. Selections]
     A new humanism: a Buddhist perspective: the university addresses of Daisaku Ikeda.
     p.   cm.
     Translated from Japanese.
     ISBN 0–8348–0334–8 (hard)   ISBN 0–8348–0367–4 (soft)
     1. Buddhism and humanism. 2. Sōka Gakkai. I. Title.
BQ4570.H8I3713   1995
294.3'928—dc20   95–449
                                       CIP

Contents

Preface

This volume is a collection of speeches and lectures I have given at universities, research institutes, and academies around the world. The earliest goes back to April 1974, when I spoke at the invitation of the University of California at Los Angeles about positive steps we can take to begin the twenty-first century in peace and with confidence in the future. Over these two decades, I have delivered a total of twenty-two talks at fifteen universities and four research institutes and academies outside Japan, and on several of those occasions I was granted an honorary degree or professorship.

There is nothing extraordinary about my knowledge or ability, but my Buddhist faith and my enduring wish for peace and a better world prevailed as I accepted each invitation to speak. I knew I would not be brilliant, but I cherished the chance to share my beliefs and ideas with others. I always prepared several months in advance, searching carefully for an appropriate theme, weighing the suitability of my arguments, scrutinizing the validity of my conclusions, and so on, until I had revised my draft many times over. Every time I finished a lecture, I felt a sense of fulfillment in having been able to convey a portion of my thoughts, and my confidence grew as I pursued each new creative challenge. This is, then, a record of sorts, narrating dimensions of my own "pilgrim's progress" over these twenty years.

In one of a volume of wrenching, powerful essays written during World War I, Romain Rolland cried out to people overcome by tyranny and war:

> Stand erect! Open your eyes and look about you! Be not afraid! The modicum of truth which you can secure by your own efforts is your safest light. Your essential need is not the acquisition of vast knowledge. The essential is that the knowledge you gain, be it little or be it much, shall be your own, nourished with your own blood, outcome of your own untrammeled effort. Freedom of the spirit is the supreme treasure. (*The Forerunners [Les Précurseurs]*, translated by Eden and Cedar Paul. London: George Allen and Unwin, Ltd., 1920, page 44.)

Rolland wrote this passage at a time when many felt that the apocalypse had struck European civilization, wreaking its fury before the eyes of a catatonic Western world. A devotee of freedom and of peace and a seeker of truth, Rolland carried out his own struggle to restore humanity and freedom of spirit with desperate intensity, thus paying tribute to his mentor, Tolstoy.

To me, this appeal is as quickening at the end of the twentieth century as it was at the beginning. It resonates the same theme that frames my lecture, "Magnificent Cosmos," which I delivered at Moscow University in May 1994.

Like Rolland and Tolstoy, I want to dedicate my life to bringing a true and generous message of encouragement, a prayer and an appeal to restore the future to humanity and let flow the bounty of the human spirit. I vow to travel the world even more energetically in this endeavor, as the twenty-first century draws nearer.

The themes of the twenty-two speeches overlap considerably, but they are roughly grouped into four sections, whose topics are culture, art, religion, and peace. Seven of these speeches have been published previously, in *A Lasting Peace,* volumes 1 and 2 (Weatherhill,

1981, 1987). They appear in this book in revised form. It is my hope that the proposals for peace, observations on history, and views of education and arts offered in these pages will have a positive effect on the thinking and life of the reader, in some way or other.

Finally, I would like to express my heartfelt appreciation for the warm welcome extended to me at the many institutions I have had the good fortune to visit. I am grateful to the translators of my speeches, and to Tsutomu Kano and Patricia Murray for their editorial help, and to all the others who have made the publication of this volume possible.

Editors' Note

Each article in this volume was prepared as a speech for delivery at a certain place and time and with a particular audience in mind. The originals were written in Japanese and later translated into English. The task of the editors was to make the minimum necessary stylistic and technical revisions in order to create internal integrity in the text. We were guided, overall, by one immediate objective: to recapture the vital moments these speeches convey in the spiritual and intellectual life of Daisaku Ikeda over roughly two decades.

As we prepared the manuscript, we had in mind a wide, general readership. For that reason, we summarized the introductory remarks—greetings, acknowledgments—that accompanied each speech. Next we established a few broad rules of style and revised accordingly, to minimize the sometimes startling differences that are unavoidable when numerous translators contribute to a single manuscript. The content was not modified, but sentence structure, paragraphing, certain grammatical usages, and terms were revised to create coherence and stylistic balance. It was also necessary to reword some expressions that, having been intended for a listening audience, were not appropriate in the printed text. We also added subheadings to help limn the topics within each speech and indicate transitions that, in speaking, are provided vocally. Finally, we realized that some of the titles of the original speeches were inappropriate as headings in a book because of their length or close resemblance to each other. With apologies to both the translators and all those who know the speeches by their original titles, we have reworded a number of the titles. We trust this will not cause confusion, however, for the place and date of each speech appear under each heading.

A great many Buddhist terms and concepts appear throughout the book. Insofar as it is intended for nonspecialist readers, we chose not to provide philosophical, etymological, or historical background for Buddhist expressions except in those cases where the author himself wished to do so. Since so many of these terms crystallize small worlds of meaning within themselves, it is often difficult or impossible to settle on a single English translation that adequately conveys all they encompass. In consideration of such constraints, for the most part we have presented the word or phrase in Japanese, described the aspects of its meaning that are relevant, and continued to use it in its Japanese form. For some terms, there are accepted English definitions that appear in dictionaries, and we used these whenever we could. As a general rule, all are discussed in context of the way they are understood in the Buddhist teachings of Nichiren.

We might have presented the articles chronologically or in another way, but we decided to group them into four chapters to bring out several dominant motifs. In writing the speeches, Mr. Ikeda sometimes drew on his previous talks, and so it was inevitable that there would be some overlap in content and supporting citations when all the speeches were compiled. Rather than trying to eliminate all repetition, we have left most of those passages as they were, since the material in question is an integral part of the particular point being argued. We hope readers will understand, therefore, that although some passages may appear to be repetitious, in each case the underlying purpose is different.

Regarding the quotations, when the original source was in a language other than English or Japanese, we tried to locate existing

English translations. When this was not possible, we had to remain content with secondary translation from the Japanese. Some of the quotations from the sutras are taken from published English works, while others are newly translated here.

This collection is intended for all interested readers regardless of their specialization, but it is hoped that it will provide grist for the mill of scholarship as well. The discussions on Buddhist traditions and thought were carefully prepared to accurately reflect current interpretations of Nichiren Buddhist ideas, as well as to offer new ways of looking at them. In such a work, it is not always possible to clarify every concept as thoroughly as the author or editors might wish. We have tried, nevertheless, to convey the same inspiration and hope that gave the original Japanese speeches their power to move human hearts and minds. If this volume can stimulate readers to rethink their ideas on humankind and the universe, its purpose will be fulfilled.

PART I

Art, Literature, and Education

Creative Life

A speech delivered at the Académie des Beaux-Arts (Academy of Fine Arts) of the Institut de France, Paris, June 14, 1989

As I reflect on the many individuals who have walked here at the Academy where I am walking now and stood where I am standing, I feel awe, respect, and an intense awareness of what the creative human being means. I have tried to express that feeling in a poem I wrote:

> Deep, deep on the remote sea floor
> lies a huge spring
> whose pure waters pour forth unceasingly,
> broader, bluer than any lake,
> flowing on with a gentle and wondrous music.
> This pure stream that has flowed
> inexhaustibly since time began,
> if we can touch it,
> we can draw upon its eternal power of life;
> if we can drink there,
> it will nourish in us unfettered powers of creativity.
> This spring that bursts forth
> from the depths of the cosmos,
> flowing into the wide sea of life,

this spring that is the mysterious source of the universe,
from its bottomless abyss
wells up the great sea of life,
and the melody of history resounds there.
That solemn and sacred music,
is it not the inner rhythm of humankind,
the language spoken by all men and women?
Can we not hear them,
the clear notes of this sacred symphony
that echo over the waves?
Can we not see it,
the pulsing rhythm that springs
from the depths of the spirit,
this profoundly deep, this unfathomable
fountain of creation?

An Integrating Force

Art is the irrepressible expression of human spirituality. So it is now, and so it has always been. Into each one of the myriad concrete forms of art is impressed the symbol of ultimate reality. The creation of a work of art takes place within spatial boundaries, but through the process of creating, the soul of the artist seeks union with that ultimate reality, what might be called cosmic life. A living work of art is life itself, born from the dynamic fusion of the self (the microcosm) and the universe (the macrocosm).

Art is to the spirit what bread is to the body; through art we find oneness with a transcendental entity, breathe its rhythm, and absorb the energy we need for spiritual renewal. Art also functions to purify the inner being, to bring the spiritual uplift that Aristotle called catharsis. What is this quality in art that has ordained it to play such an elemental and enduring role in human life? I believe it is the power to integrate, to reveal the wholeness of things. In an early scene of *Faust,* Goethe has Faust rapturously declare, "Into the whole how all things blend, each in the other working, living."[1] If we accept this marvelous statement of the interconnection of all living things, then art becomes the elemental modality through which humans discover their bonds with humans, humanity with nature, and humanity with the universe.

Whether it is poetry, painting, or music, a jewel of artistic expression can stir within us an ineffable impulse that carries us soaring through the empyrean, letting us share the experience with others while confirming its reality. Art's force of integration works in living beings by opening the way for the finite to become infinite, for the specificity of actual experience to assume universal meaning. Religion has always worked through art to affirm identity with the universal, as we can see in the intertwining of art and religious ritual in ancient drama. The English author Jane E. Harrison writes, "It is at the outset one and the same impulse that sends a man to church and to the theatre."2

According to an anecdote I once heard, a Japanese actor sensed that impulse when he made a trip to Europe many years ago. During a visit to the Louvre, after seeing a number of masterpieces of Western art, he was asked about his impressions. His immediate observation was, "Everything is so Christian!" Such a reaction, though overstated, conveys honest surprise at how pervasively the spirit of Western art has been nourished by the Christian tradition. To observe how "Christian" the art seemed was perhaps the way this visitor from Asia, thrust into the heartland of Western art, tried to express his encounter with the ultimate reality he sensed there. The cathedrals of Notre Dame and Chartres, a summation in architecture of the worldview of medieval Christianity, embodied the awesome power of art to integrate the world's reality and ultimate reality. In the Middle Ages, art was religion, and religion was art, and in the fusion of the two, people carried out their passionate quest for a more fulfilling life.

Connecting Space

Compared with the rigorous monotheism of Christianity, Japan's religious tradition is vague and undefined in many areas, but there is a strong esthetic dimension in Japanese religiosity that forms a link with the universal. The French writer André Malraux, one of the great minds of the postwar world, understood that dimension. He saw the traditional Japanese esthetic as different from the Western, calling it an "inner reality." That insight reflects his clear sense of the religious motivation behind the Japanese perception of unity, of common life, in nature and the universe. Somewhat earlier, another French intellectual, Paul Claudel, compared Western and Japanese esthetics; he described the latter as concerned with becoming one with nature rather than dominating it. An inclination to reach out for wholeness, whether it is conscious or not, permeates all of Japanese culture.

For some time now, the force of integration that once infused art and religion in both Eastern and Western civilizations has been waning as modernization overtakes us. Since the end of the nineteenth century, people sensitive enough to see this coming have been issuing warnings, and I do not wish to rehearse them here. But when human beings cut themselves off from nature and the universe, their bonds with each other also shrivel and die. The consequence is that people are isolated and alone; worse, this situation has become so "normal" that it is not even recognized as a problem.

The environment of art, also, has steadily been transformed as the modern era moves onward. Think of contemporary theatre compared with the classical age of Greek drama, when the audience, gathered in the amphitheater around the stage, sometimes participated in plays more enthusiastically than the actors themselves. Today, when a solitary artist faces a blank piece of paper or white canvas, how can he or she connect with the unknown audience? No matter how talented the artist, the environment today offers no area of mutual encounter, no organic community of interest where the integrating force of art can work to connect us with ultimate reality.

Some people seek to rescue a dying, prehistoric vitality, trying to rediscover the stout hardiness of ancient people. Others dream of a rugged, indomitable nature unfettered by modernization. The struggle to regain wholeness takes many forms. On the other hand, since late in the last century, it sometimes seems as though the very troubles themselves of each era have brought forth a galaxy of stars marching past in an opulent parade of brilliant minds. While today there is greater possibility than ever before of freedom and artistic diversity, we find the ability to transcend the visible and penetrate ever deeper into reality weakening, and the yearning to heal disconnected spirits drying up.

Connected with Totality

The idea of integration is expressed in the Buddhist term *kechi-en* (literally to "join" a "connection," it denotes a causal relationship or a function that joins life and its environment). The concept arises from the theory of "dependent origination," a philosophical construct important in Buddhism since the time of Shakyamuni. The theory of dependent origination holds that every phenomenon, be it social or natural, is the result of its connection with something else. Nothing can exist in total isolation; everything is interrelated. Usually we think of interactions in spatial terms, but the Buddhist conception is multidimensional, including the dimension of time. At the source of the Japanese esthetic consciousness of empathy and coexistence with nature, which appealed to both Claudel and Malraux, is a primitive animism, but even more, an outlook rooted in the Buddhist concept of dependent origination.

Traditional art forms such as the tea ceremony, flower arranging, gardens, decorated sliding doors, or folding screens are not created to have inherent value or meaning on their own. They derive their full meaning only when placed in a "space" at the heart of ordinary, everyday life. Their value is dependent on *kechi-en,* the connection they establish with the space around them. Traditional forms of Japanese poetry, also, such as *renga* (linked verse) and *haiku,* could not have come into being without a space where many people could gather and literally bring out connections among the place, themselves, and their verses.

In Mahayana Buddhism the term *ku* (sometimes glossed as emptiness or void) describes the reality of all things as arising from *kechi-en.* There is still a tendency even today to associate the idea of *ku* with the notion of nothingness. Buddhism, particularly Hinayana

Buddhism, is itself partially responsible. Hinayana thought encourages a kind of nihilism through the idea that enlightenment is sought via the negation of worldly value. Mahayana Buddhism places the concept of *ku* in a framework quite different from this static, nihilistic understanding. Mahayana Buddhists see reality as being in eternal flux; it is the flowing movement of life itself. The philosophy of Henri Bergson, in which reality is found in the continuity of phenomena rather than their eternal character, is actually closer to the Mahayana ideal than Hinayana Buddhism is.

I call the dynamism that ceaselessly pulsates through the Mahayana idea of *ku* "creative life." Creative life is devoted entirely to transcending the individual self by continually reaching beyond the limits of space and time in pursuit of the universal self. The creative life makes a new breakthrough, achieves self-renewal, every day, always attuned to the original rhythm of the universe, and by so doing it brings about a complete transformation. Ten years ago, a volume containing conversations I held with René Huyghe of the Académie Française was published. There, Huyghe arrived at the heart of Mahayana Buddhism when he described its essence as "spiritual life," which he explained by saying that, "We are connected with the totality . . . [and] united with the creative action of the future, toward which the universe advances."[3]

The Sutra of this World

The Lotus Sutra, the core of Mahayana teaching, describes the dynamism of creative life in a number of ways to allow a comprehensive understanding of what it means. In one respect, creative life is free of the bounds of time and space, free to expand and grow. At the same time, creative life in all its expansiveness is contained within a single moment of an individual life. The first part of the Lotus Sutra explains how all phenomena reveal the fundamental Law (the ultimate reality of the universe). When we become one with the Law, we can recognize that all phenomena are condensed within our life, and at the same time our life pervades the universe. In the latter part of the sutra, the Buddha is presented as having no beginning or end, revealing thereby the eternal nature of life. Furthermore, past and future are contained in the present moment (since the present is the effect of the past-as-cause as well as being the cause of effect in the future). As a whole, the Lotus Sutra elucidates the dynamism of creative life, which knowing no bound or restriction, is free of the fetters of space and time.

On the level of our everyday activities, creative life propels us to the uninhibited realization of self-perfection. What sets the Lotus Sutra apart from other sutras is its immediate focus; it places the quest to realize the Way of the Bodhisattva right here, in the midst of the troubled, mundane world. It leads us to elevate ourselves, transcend our "lesser self," and affirm the universal self here, now, in the middle of ordinary reality:

The Lotus Sutra is rich in picturesque, dramatic, and literary images. The middle section contains a description of the Ceremony in the Air, in which an enormous Treasure Tower decorated with seven kinds of jewels (including gold, silver, lapis lazuli, and pearls) appears in the sky. Rising high in the universe, it symbolizes the grandeur and dignity of life. In the chapter "The Life Span of the Thus Come One," the peaceful world is described as a land constantly filled with gods and men:

> The halls and pavilions in its gardens and groves are adorned with various kinds of gems. Jeweled trees abound in flowers and fruit where living beings enjoy themselves at ease. The gods strike heavenly drums, constantly making many kinds of music. Manadrava blossoms rain down, scattering over the Buddha and the great assembly.[4]

Painting, music, and poetic images vie to evoke a truly wonderful world. There are times when art and religion can be mutually antagonistic, but in the Lotus Sutra they harmonize with and complement each other.

The Metaphor of Dance

The unfolding of creative life according to the Lotus Sutra, then, encompasses all the dimensions of human life—in Kierkegaardian terms, the religious, ethical, and esthetic dimensions. They come together to form a whole, a dynamic cosmic current that, as it is refined and clarified again and again, calls up the image of a multicolored top spinning faster and faster until finally all colors are blended into a single, breathtaking hue. There is a passage that simply and beautifully captures the essence of the Lotus Sutra:

> Although you are not the Venerable Mahakashyapa, you should leap for joy! Although you are not Shariputra, you should rise and dance! When Bodhisattva Jogyo emerged from the earth, he leapt forth joyfully. . . . [5]

Mahakashyapa and Shariputra, who personify intelligence, were among Shakyamuni's preeminent disciples. Here, "dance" is the metaphor for the joy they felt upon hearing the teachings of the Lotus Sutra. They projected the joy of life that comes from embracing the ultimate reality of the universe and the highest value in humanity. Bodhisattva Jogyo was at the head of the countless multitudes of bodhisattvas whom Shakyamuni called forth from within the earth when he expounded the Lotus Sutra, the multitudes who were entrusted with propagating the Law after Shakyamuni's death.

"Leap for joy," "rise and dance," "leapt forth joyfully" are strong artistic images filled with Buddhist symbolism suggesting the vigorous life and energy of the bodhisattvas appearing out of the earth. They convey the vibrant dynamism of creative life. As I use the word "symbol," I am thinking of the brilliant tradition of symbolism in French literature. In the Lotus Sutra, too, since it may be read as the drama of the cycle of an individual life, the metaphor of dancing is meant less to project a concrete image than to symbolize the sublimity of creative life. Hence the image of wave upon wave of bodhisattvas springing forth symbolizes the supreme joy in the profound human quest to achieve harmony with the fundamental Law of the universe and the fulfillment in ceaseless striving to contribute to human society.

The simple beauty of the metaphor of dance calls to mind a passage by Paul Valéry in a dialogue in *Dance and the Soul*. There, Valéry has Socrates remark, upon seeing a dancing woman:

. . . while this exaltation and vibration of life, while this supremacy of tension, and this whirling into the greatest agility humanly possible, have the virtues and powers of flame; and that the shames, the worries, the sillinesses, and the monotonous fare of existence are consumed in it, making a shining light in our eyes of what is divine in a mortal woman? [6]

Valéry's passage is rendered in a genre quite different from the Buddhist sutra. Yet both use the metaphor of dance as a way to put such inexpressible purity of movement into language and to form an image of the divine nature of art.

Spiritual Revolution

We live in an era of unparalleled difficulty and change. In times like these, people begin to look inward, and that is happening today. Toward the end of his life, haunted by the tramp of army boots over France and the rest of Europe, Valéry tried to launch a "spiritual league" of people dedicated to higher goals. André Malraux, also, was certain he sensed signs of a spiritual revolution that would take place in the coming century. They saw the glimmerings of what we have called creative life, that force which will grow and flower into an articulated movement. Through inner human revolution, it will surge onward, carried by the imperative behind the "spiritual league" and the "spiritual revolution," the quest for ultimate reality. I believe that this is the wellspring of the energy that activates all of human endeavor, including art. Let me conclude with another of my poems, this one composed in honor of art.

> Art,
> O eternal light,
> imperishable imprint of civilizations!
> Hymn to life,
> to liberty, to creation, to joy!
> Intense prayer,
> profound harmony with the fundamental reality!

Forum of friendship,
where millions of beings
join with, greet, and smile at each other.
A man of letters declared in the West:
"East is East and West is West,
but when the two giants meet
boundaries and nationalities will disappear."
At the same time, in the East, a great poet wrote:
"East and West must marry
on the altar of humanity."
And here is Art,
inviting the soul by reaching her hand out
toward a soothing and serene wood,
toward a garden where imagination blazes across
    the sky;
inviting it to the noble stage of wisdom
and leading it toward the far-off horizon
of universal civilization.

NOTES

1. J.W. Goethe, *Faust, A Tragedy* trans. Bayard Taylor (New York: The Modern Library, 1967), 17–18.

2. Jane Ellen Harrison, *Ancient Art and Ritual* (Oxford: Oxford University Press, 1951), 9.

3. René Huyghe and Daisaku Ikeda, *Dawn After Dark,* trans. by Richard L. Gage (New York: Weatherhill, Inc., 1991), 224 and 337–8.

4. *The Lotus Sutra,* trans. Burton Watson (Columbia University Press, 1993), 230–31.

5. Gosho Translation Committee, ed. and trans., *The Major Writings of Nichiren Daishonin,* (Tokyo: NSIC, 1988), 5:161.

6. Paul Valéry, "Dance and the Soul," from *Paul Valéry: An Anthology,* ed. Jackson Mathews. (Princeton: Princeton University Press, 1977), 299.

The Kemalist Revolution: A Model

A speech delivered at Ankara University, Turkey,
June 24, 1992

I am deeply grateful to receive an honorary doctorate from Ankara University, an academic institution with a long and distinguished tradition, founded by the first president of the Republic of Turkey and "father of the Turks," Mustafa Kemal Atatürk. It is also an honor to have been invited to speak today, and I would like to thank the university rector, Dr. Serin, the members of the university, and the many distinguished guests who have gathered here.

A Japanese scholar who was very knowledgeable about Turkey once referred to it as "distant, yet close." The two countries are separated by a vast geographical distance, one being located by the Mediterranean sea and the other off the eastern shore of the Eurasian continent. Yet, surprisingly, there are cultural and ethnic affinities between the two. Three months ago, I met Professor Nur Yalman, an eminent Turkish cultural anthropologist currently teaching at Harvard University. He reminded me of several parallels between our homelands. First there is evidence dating far back into prehistory that points to similar racial origins for Japanese and Turks in Central Asia. Also, our countries were situated at either extremity of the Silk Road, which was for centuries a medium of cultural and commercial exchange between different peoples. Perhaps for this reason, there are some unexpected similarities in the languages, customs, and traditions of Turkey and Japan even today. In Professor Yalman's words, we are "natural allies."

The Turkish people place a great deal of importance on friendship. Perhaps that is best symbolized by the word for comradeship, *arkadaçlik,* but fidelity and courage are also central in their value system. A vibrant brand of universalism and humanism is very apparent in Turkey. That spirit is crystallized in two lines written by the poet Yunus Emre, whose words resound with force and clarity across seven centuries:

> I am not here on earth for strife,
> Love is the mission of my life.[1]

The world faces an extraordinary drama of change in the closing years of the twentieth century. The establishment of a new and peaceful international order will mean replacing the hard power of economic, military, and political instruments with new tools of soft power such as systems, laws, information, and peaceful negotiation. In his lecture at Soka University in 1990, Rector Serin pointed out that we are seeing the transition from an age of absolute and monolithic authority and ideology to an age in which decisions are made through the collective wisdom of the people. I believe that the way to peace lies in extending and strengthening the international system already in place, albeit in nascent and imperfect form, the core of which is the United Nations. To build a new international order based on peace, we must encourage strong support from the public around the world. Furthermore, we need a spiritual foundation, or *zeitgeist,* that will let the new system function well. Our organization, Soka Gakkai International, in its capacity as an NGO (non-governmental organization), is trying to do its part by consistently supporting the objectives of the United Nations.

The Themes of Kemalism

I would now like to talk about some of the underlying themes of Kemalism, which can be considered the national philosophy of modern Turkey. Coined after Kemal Atatürk, who developed its principle concepts as a base for his sweeping reform, the essence of Kemalism is much more than a type of Westernization. It represents, rather, a remarkable series of choices coming out of Turkey's long and extraordinarily rich historical experience as a witness to the rise and fall of many cultures and civilizations. Kemalism is the product of a land that is at a central crossroads of our globe. The great city known to the world at different times as Byzantium, Constantinople, and Istanbul is a fitting symbol of this meeting of East and West.

The six principles of Kemalism are: (1) republicanism, (2) nationalism, (3) populism, (4) statism, (5) secularism, and (6) reformism. They constitute a framework that is filled with and held firm by openness of spirit and striving toward the universal. Kemal Atatürk's overriding desire and goal was to awaken the Turkish people to their potential in the modern world. As his motto "make new friends, but treasure old ones" suggests, he successfully avoided the pitfalls of parochial nationalism in seeking to open his nation and his people to the world, and in so doing he proclaimed the universal nature of his vision.

Both Kemal Atatürk as a man and Kemalism as a set of principles demonstrate a coherent and developed sense of balance and proportion, a trait that has proved to be highly effective. Atatürk the valiant reformer was given at times to explosive passions, but his actions were always governed by a will of steel and a strong sense of moderation. The annals of world history would have to be searched exhaustively to find another individual who could remain as self-possessed and in control through the upheaval that accompanied such a momentous attempt at reform as Turkey's. By its massive scope, depth, and thoroughness, it compared, in the words of Arnold Toynbee, to "the Renaissance, the Reformation, the secularist, scientific [revolution]... the French Revolution, and the Industrial Revolution...telescoped into a single lifetime. . . ."[2] And while Atatürk was bringing new life to his country, his contemporaries Hitler, Mussolini, and Stalin gave in to the dark temptation of domination and brought instead untold suffering as they tumbled to destruction.

Atatürk was intensely conscious of the demonic nature of power, particularly because the scale and scope of his own were so great. During the last years of his life, understanding the pitfalls of so much concentrated authority, he tried to abolish the one-party system and deliberately create an opposition. The effort proved premature, but the move to voluntarily relinquish absolute power was heroic and virtually unique in modern history.

Atatürk was also able to balance the merits of each situation, even if he seemed to contradict himself. For example, the last years of the Ottoman empire left him with bitter memories, and he was extremely wary of foreign investment or interference in Turkish affairs, to the extent that to some he seemed xenophobic. Yet he welcomed teachers and instructors from other countries. His enlightened approach to education, to name only one area, bore all the hallmarks of his moderation and restraint—certainly not passionate antiforeignism. He also had the foresight to focus on long-term developments and to steer clear, for example, of any pan-Turkish ambitions. Having secured the borders and territory of the new-born state, he never used military force against any of his neighbors.

We who live in this day and age urgently need the qualities of character that Atatürk had. The concerns of people in the contemporary world increasingly are transnational and global, and they demand moderation and restraint. We can no longer afford to let dogmatic or parochial views inform our actions; we must develop the ability to see ourselves objectively with respect to the rest of the world. Only those with farsighted open-mindedness can aspire to globalism. The ability to strike a balance between one's own interests and those of other nations—or, at a deeper level, between the individual and the universal—is the mark of the world citizen. In the long run, these are the qualities that must become the spiritual foundation for the rules and structures of a just international order.

Ismet Inönü succeeded Atatürk as president of Turkey. During his tenure, and in accordance with the will of his predecessor, Turkey established a multiparty system and carried out a democratic transfer of power. Arnold Toynbee celebrated this event as "a notable triumph for a sense of fair play and moderation in politics,"[3] the essential components of the open spirit and universalist thrust of Kemalism.

On the People's Side

Like Atatürk himself, Kemalism stands for the well-being of the people. A philosophy that is truly universal does not hover in some abstract limbo; it penetrates the hearts, souls, and lives of the people. Transmitted from heart to heart, it crosses borders to unify the world. Humanity itself is the soil from which universality springs.

Now and then I try to express my feelings in poetry. Let me quote one part of a verse I wrote to celebrate ordinary, common people:

> People!
> you alone are reality
> outside of you there is no real world
> ......
> Science without you is coldhearted
> philosophy without you is barren
> art without you is empty
> religion without you is merciless [4]

My attempt at poetry is paltry compared with the moving, famous speech that Atatürk delivered before the National Assembly in August 1926. In that speech, he proclaimed:

> Every great movement must find its source in the depths of a people's soul, the original spring of all strengths and greatness. Failing this, all is ruin and dust.

The unflagging confidence of his words grew, no doubt, from his unparalleled record of achievement as a leader deeply engaged with and committed to the people. Whether in battle, or in the less lethal arenas of politics and education, he always fought alongside his countrymen, sharing their suffering and joys and urging them to greater awareness and pride as Turks. Through his brave and dedicated efforts, he gave new courage to a country exhausted and despondent from war. He revolutionized the consciousness of a nation, directing popular energy toward the construction of a new Turkey. In doing this, he rescued his nation from a crisis that threatened its very existence.

The transformation Atatürk led in his country is possible in other countries, as well. When it happens, and when people of all countries feel the same healthy pride in their identity, they will emerge as world citizens. This outlook does not submerge ethnic distinctions; rather, it enhances the unique qualities of each society. People who have been awakened to their global responsibilities will join hands in universal solidarity, each in their own way contributing their special assets.

Education is the precondition for spiritual unification, and it was a priority under Atatürk. Insofar as education was one of its major pillars, the Kemalist revolution was not radical, though on the surface it might have appeared to be. That it took, in fact, a gradualist approach may have been the factor that ensured the success of the revolution.

The process of sublimation that leads to a wider, more universal perception of the world operates through the interaction and mutual stimulation of peoples and cultures, namely, through education. I use this term in the broadest sense, including dialogue as a mode of learning. The words of Professor Yalman remind us that education is the most direct and certain path to the universal and hence, to world peace. It is certainly education that lets us transcend different backgrounds and discover commonalities. It enables us to think on a higher plane, that is, as human beings; to free ourselves from thinking that is based solely on membership in a particular faction or school.

The Kemalist revolution was a cultural transformation of great scope and depth, but nowhere was it more successful than in the area of educational reform. Atatürk used education to create a "new Turkey" and a "new Turkish people." Among all his achievements, this was accomplished with an earthy practicality and personal engagement that were noble, idealistic, and very effective. I have an image of the first president, blackboard and chalk in hand, traveling to all corners of the new republic to teach his countrymen the romanized Turkish alphabet that he himself had devised.

Citizens of the Nation, Citizens of the World

Behind all he achieved at the national level is Atatürk's view of civilization. He saw it in terms of its universal values. In 1921, speaking of the need to eliminate deep-rooted enmity between ethnic groups, Atatürk stated:

> It is not by military victories that we shall do this, but only by reaching for everything that modern knowledge and civilization demand, and by actually attaining the cultural level realized by all civilized peoples. [5]

Atatürk believed in the ideal of cultural progress to instill global values. It was the force that would enable the Turkish people to become good citizens of their nation, and thereby to become good citizens of the world. His ideas predate the eclipse of the Europe-centered positivist view of history, perhaps best articulated in Oswald Spengler's *The Decline of the West* (1923). While Spengler saw civilization as moving along an inevitable, linear path, our experience of history has provided ample proof that civilization moves in ways that are not simple, linear, or inevitable. Furthermore, the influence of Western values has been undermined by new theories in anthropology developed in this century. The paradigm of cultural relativism, which rejects hierarchical evaluation of cultures and civilizations, has been particularly influential.

Atatürk, however, remained firmly convinced that the process of cultural enhancement would enable the Turkish people to realize higher, global values as world citizens. In other words, his thinking is characterized by his aspiration toward the universal. With fresh ideas and an open heart, he sought a new place in history for his beloved homeland.

Many students of Atatürk's life share my belief that his policies were guided not simply by hypothetical ideals but by a specific historical model. If any, it is probably the French Revolution, which Atatürk studied intensely during his youth. Let us say, then, that France and the French people of that time provided the model for Turkey's new Constitution and its educational system. The twentieth-century French philosopher Simone Weil described the universal appeal of revolutionary France:

> The Revolution melted all the peoples subject to the French Crown into one single mass...by their enthusiasm for national sovereignty. Those who had been Frenchmen by force, became so by free consent; many of those who were not French wanted to become so.[6]

Replace "France" with "Turkey" in this passage, and we have an idea of Atatürk's vision of a new Turkish people.

In recent years, Turkey has become the focus of growing attention for its role as a meeting place of Eastern and Western civilizations. This stems from more than economic interests or religious and ethnic ties with other countries. Rather, it indicates the universal appeal of the enlightened philosophy of Kemalism. It is very likely that the spirit of the Turkish national motto, "Peace at Home, Peace Abroad" will inspire other countries as they deal with the volatile international context of our times. I can envision an enchanting, peaceful future when many peoples, including Japanese, will be able to travel a new Silk Road of cultural exchange and mutual understanding. This will be a channel for individuals to share and deepen their appreciation of the universal values of human dignity, harmony with nature, and responsibility to future generations. Those values will equip us with the means to resolve the complex global problems before us. I, too, pledge to do my utmost to help achieve this milestone in the quest for world peace.

I will conclude with an expression of hope and resolve by Yunus Emre that in two lines articulates my feelings better than I could ever do:

{ The world to me is sustenance,
Its peoples and my own are one.[7]]

NOTES

1. Talat Sait Halam, *The Humanist Poetry of Yunus Emre* (Istanbul: Istanbul Matbaasi, 1972), 78.

2. Arnold Toynbee, *The World and the West* (London: Oxford University Press, 1953), 28.

3. Ibid., 29.

4. Daisaku Ikeda, *The People,* in *Songs from My Heart,* trans. Burton Watson (New York & Tokyo: John Weatherhill Inc., 1978), 75–76.

5. David Hotham, *The Turks* (London: John Murray Ltd.,1972), 24.

6. Simone Weil, *The Need for Roots* (London: Ark Paperbacks, 1987), 105.

7. Yunus Emre, *The City of the Heart: Yunus Emre's Verses of Wisdom and Love,* trans. Suhasaiz (Rockport: Element Books, 1992), 59.

A Matter of the Heart

A speech delivered at Peking University, Beijing,
May 28, 1990

It is a pleasure to be here at Peking University once again and to meet so many members of the faculty and student body. This is my sixth visit, and your warm hospitality has always made me feel very welcome. This time, I am deeply honored to be the first recipient of the Outstanding Education Award from Peking University. I am also privileged to serve here as advisor to the center for Japanese Studies and will do everything in my power to support the continued growth and development of this university.

Let me take this opportunity to express my sincere thanks for the understanding and cooperation of all those involved in the exchange program between Soka University and Peking University. As you may know, Soka University is the first Japanese institution to engage in scholarly exchange with Peking University. This program is the fruit of the friendship and good will of China and Peking University. On behalf of the faculty, staff, and students at Soka University, I bring warm regards.

Ancient China and Greece

Many years ago I decided to make education my lifework. It is people who will pave the way toward the future of our world, and there is no greater influence in the development of an individual than that of solid, human-centered education. Learning is the fundamental force that builds society and shapes an age. It nurtures and tempers the infinite potential latent in all of us, and it directs our energies toward the creation of values.

Today, knowledge is increasingly specialized and compartmentalized. To integrate and coordinate knowledge has always required wisdom, far-sightedness, and character, but perhaps now more than ever. In times such as ours when the contemporary world is on the verge of an unprecedented surge of internationalism, education is crucial and can only become more so, not only for the future of individual nations, but for the world as a whole.

In the years to come, it will be especially important that education have a firm philosophical foundation. The glorious tradition of pedagogical thought for which China is justly famous may, therefore, turn out to be an invaluable asset. That tradition represents a great river moving with tremendous, focused energy toward the fulfillment of human potential. Of all peoples, the ancient Greeks and the Chinese possessed by far the deepest wisdom regarding education. Both had a precise and profound grasp of the ideas and curricula necessary for the cultivation of character and the elevation of humanity.

For Greeks in the classical era, one of the main educational goals was the development of individuality. This meant not simply inculcating the young with received knowledge, but also developing their latent potential. The Greek emphasis on the self-activation of the learner is illustrated in the method of dialogue, developed by Plato and used at the Academy in Athens to help students find the path to understanding and to encourage individuality.

In East Asia, educational ideas that originated in China flourished throughout the entire region and its peripheries. Ancient China produced many gifted philosophers who traveled far and wide preaching the Way. Even when they lost all hope for integrity in government, they continued to devote themselves to educating the young. For these thinkers, the point of education was not so much teaching or instructing but cultivating and fostering.

The teachers of antiquity demanded from their students both self-discipline and an unquenchable motivation to learn. A passage in Confucius's *Analects* reads:

> I do not open up the truth to one who is not eager to get knowledge, nor help out anyone who is not anxious to explain himself. When I have presented one corner of a subject to anyone, and he cannot learn the other three from it, I do not repeat my lesson.[1]

It is instructive that the Chinese word for "learning" is made up of two characters, one for "study" and the other for "question," suggesting that the ancient sages gave equal weight to both activities and thereby encouraged dialogue. Their approach to the concepts "opening up the truth to the individual" stems from a deep insight into human nature and embodies the genius of the Chinese educational model.

In recent years, Western scholars have shown growing interest in the roots of East Asian learning. Columbia University professor William Theodore de Bary, in his book *The Liberal Tradition in China,* traces the evolution of liberalism in Chinese philosophy. He points out that the spirit of mutual support and enlightenment that characterizes Chinese scholarship was cultivated by a method of study that depended on discussion and the sharing of ideas.

One of the central aspects of the educational systems in both ancient Greece and China is the constant focus on human beings. As Rousseau so astutely noted about the Greek myths, they tell the story not of how human beings shed blood for the sake of the gods, but of how the gods struggled for the sake of humanity. In China, the sages were even less interested in gods, it seems. They categorically rejected the idea of the supernatural. Confucius himself "did not talk of extraordinary things, feats of strength, disorders and spiritual beings."[2]

From Knowledge, Tranquillity

A second crucial insight of the ancients regarding education was their recognition of the need for a firm moral stand. The cultivation of the

inner person was central in their priorities, but they did not stop
there; they argued with equal vehemence the need to examine the
practicalities of government and the welfare of the people. It is significant that one of the greatest works of Plato was entitled *The Republic*. This masterpiece focused on the role of the human psyche, social
hierarchy, and the imperative for justice in the construction of the
ideal state. Plato continued to be intensely concerned with politics
until the last years of his life. In the Chinese tradition, also, knowledge
was regarded as an essential precondition for peace. This sentiment is
clearly expressed in the fifth chapter of the *Great Learning:*

> Things being investigated, knowledge became complete. Their
> knowledge being complete, their thoughts were sincere. Their
> thoughts being sincere, their hearts were then rectified. Their
> hearts being rectified, the persons were cultivated. Their per-
> sons being cultivated, their families were regulated. Their fami-
> lies being regulated, their States were rightly governed. Their
> States being rightly governed, the whole kingdom was made
> tranquil and happy.[3]

The ideas of Plato, Aristotle, and the other great Greek thinkers
were not passed down only within the historical legacy of Greece;
they survived as part of the intellectual heritage of Western civilization as a whole. Similarly, the teachings of the Chinese sages
formed the ethos of a great civilization embracing vast territories
and a huge population, whose philosophical underpinnings were
carried through more than three millennia. That devotion to
human learning is not confined to Confucianism, and it has
evolved into an unfaltering quest to create cosmos (order) out of
chaos (disorder) through the process of education.

China's great river of tradition carries with it many ideas that,
even today, deserve critical attention. Ming-dynasty philosopher
Wang Yangming believed that the foundation for cultural development and a stable society had to be sought in the people themselves.
Similarly, in the latter seventeenth century Huang Zongxi wrote *A
Plan for the Prince* during the tumultuous period of transition mark-
ing the end of the Ming and the beginning of the Qing dynasties in

the mid 1600s. In his book, he argued for autonomy of schools and for promotion of officials on the basis of personal merit and ability.

These ideas were not, of course, fully realized. The Confucian emphasis in education led to the creation of a system of fiercely competitive civil service examinations, which put much learning out of the reach of most people. Confucian learning was always monopolized by the ruling class and did not penetrate far among ordinary people, but even so, the influence of the ancient educational system remains strong among the Chinese people. Chinese education encapsulates a sense of order and history; coupled with the perception of the universe developed in this system, it is directed toward the creation of a new cosmic order through the self-perfection of human character. The same orientation emerges in the Chinese interpretation of Marxist thought as the basis for eternal revolution. Perhaps this tradition of seeking cosmic order in the perfection of human character will become the wellspring of what Sinologist Leon Vandermeersch of the University of Paris described as the "new Chinese-ideograph culture sphere." The latter, he believes, will become the foundation of a civilization comparable to that of the West.

It has been suggested that the Copernican revolution destroyed the medieval image of the world but did not provide a new image to replace it. Instead, it launched an age that lacked a worldview. Today, we are entering the twilight years of the post-Copernican age. In this time of change, I believe, the spiritual heritage of China, where pedagogy plays such a major role, will make a tremendous contribution in the formation of a new worldview resting on the twin foundations of universalism and humanism.

Toward Sino-Japanese Friendship

Today, we are trying to formulate a new chapter in the relationship between China and Japan. It is a time for us in Japan to reassess our posture toward our great neighbor to the west. I hardly need mention the tremendous cultural debt that my country owes China, not only in educational philosophy, but in every other cultural dimension as well. How can we repay such a debt? There can be no question that for Japan, the awareness of how much we owe China will be an important element in exchange between the two nations.

In this age of globalism, neither individuals nor countries can survive in isolation. Inasmuch as we are all part of the same world, we will incur obligations to countless other people and to countless other nations. Obligation is the essence of humanity. It is the manifestation of the spirituality that sustains and lubricates the workings of human society. In this vein, the early twentieth-century writer Lü Xun who taught at Beijing University in its early years recorded his memories of Gonkuro Fujino, his mentor when he was studying medicine in Japan. In his book entitled *Fujino Sensei* (*Professor Fujino*), he wrote that once someone incurs a debt, that person carries it throughout life. A debt is essentially a "matter of the heart" that concerns the recipient rather than the giver. The feelings of obligation and attachment to his teacher come through powerfully in this great Chinese novelist's work. In them I sense the clear reverberation of humanity's loftiest spirit.

It is important to possess a sense of obligation and to repay our debts. That is why I believe that Japan must devote its best efforts to the development and well-being of China, a country to which it owes an incalculable cultural debt. China and Japan are geographically near, separated only by a narrow strip of water, and they have been linked by close ties since ancient times. We share a long tradition of friendship and there is much promise that we can work together to forge a dynamic and genuine era of peace and stability. Such a partnership will contribute not only to our own welfare, but to the cause of peace in Asia and the entire world.

Friendship is proved genuine through steadfastness and fidelity. Sino-Japanese amity today will develop into true friendship by staunch loyalty on the part of both countries. No matter what issues might come between us, the bonds of friendship must never be broken. I believe that our most important task now is to establish firm foundations for a sturdy bridge to the future. Political and economic exchange will be important, but the ties joining the hearts of the peoples of both countries are even more so. Without trust between the Japanese and Chinese peoples, political and economic ties and diplomatic agreements will be nothing more than castles in the sand. The "ships" of state and commerce will sail in safety only if they are buoyed up and carried by the "seas" of the people.

The bonds of affection between peoples are invisible, making them strong; they are intangible, making them universal and enduring. Such bonds are made possible by the splendor of culture urging the human spirit toward eternity and universality. Education, meanwhile, opens up the infinite potential of the human soul and nurtures the bonds of equality and fellowship. Cultural and educational exchange will provide the basis for truly eternal ties between our two peoples. Toward that end, I repeat my call for more extensive exchange between China and Japan to open the way for a second, even more vigorous stream of exchange over our treasured bridge of culture.

In 1998, Peking University will celebrate its centennial. As it enters its second century, its role in the world as one of the oldest and most respected East Asian institutions of higher learning will be more vital than ever before. Part of the motto of Peking University is the phrase "creation of the new." This echoes the idea of *soka* or "creation of value" that is part of the name Soka Gakkai. Inspired by the glorious vision of the new world that this university will help create, I promise to redouble my efforts for increasingly fruitful ties between our university and yours, our country and yours.

NOTES

1. *The Chinese Classics: Confucian Analects,* trans. James Legge (Taiwan: SMC Publishing Inc., 1991), 197.

2. Ibid., 201.

3. *The Chinese Classics: The Great Learning,* trans. James Legge (Taiwan: SMC Publishing Inc., 1991), 358–59.

Beyond the Profit Motive

A speech delivered at the University of the Philippines,
April 10, 1991

I would like to thank Dr. Abueva, distinguished president of the University of the Philippines; Dr. Roman, the chancellor; Dr. Agulto, dean of the College of Business Administration; and the other faculty members in attendance today for inviting me to speak at this venerable institution with such a proud tradition of scholarship.

Let me also congratulate all the students graduating today. Their commencement coincides with the seventy-fifth anniversary of the establishment of the business administration course. As all of you, students and faculty, support the ideals of world citizenship espoused by that great Filipino hero José Rizal, I would like to share with you some of my thoughts on his vision.

The Spirit of Fairness

I have long cherished the saying, "Control your business; don't let it control you." By its very nature, business is geared to economic efficiency and the pursuit of profit. A businessman who works strictly for the good of his enterprise alone will think only in terms of the bottom line. That narrow focus has given rise on occasion to competition so excessive as to blow up in military conflict. If business activities are to contribute to efforts toward peace, the logic of capital must be tempered by the logic of humanity. How can this be achieved? In Japan, there is a term *kosei,* which may be translated as the spirit of fairness. It also means equality and impartiality, as well as justice. I was interested to learn that the term *katarungan* in Tagalog also contains these two meanings of justice and equality.

A person with the spirit of fairness recognizes the inherent contradiction in economic activity that makes the rich richer and the poor even poorer, both on the individual and national levels. Such a person clearly recognizes the insidious threat of economic growth that thrives at the expense of the global environment and the delicate balance of the ecosystem. The "export" of pollution to countries with less strict regulations for example, is anathema to people who place justice and equality first. Japanese may provide a case in point; in this regard they need to think long and hard about their activities abroad.

The spirit of fairness or justice is not an *a priori* condition. When Dr. Abueva spoke at Soka University in 1990, he described the traditional Filipino spirit of *bayanihan* (mutual help in communal societies). Such patterns of ensuring the well-being of everyone are cultivated and handed down through the trials of history. By tough challenges, the spirit of fairness is transformed from the ethos of a people into a universal principle endowed with the strength of steel, the warmth of the sun, and the vastness of the sky.

One such ordeal is rendered in the trenchant war novel, *Without Seeing the Dawn,* written by Stevan Javellana, an alumnus of the University of the Philippines. Reading this book, I was painfully reminded of the atrocities committed by the Imperial Army and Navy during the Pacific War, and, as a Japanese citizen, I offer my profound apologies. As one who fervently wishes to help construct the foundation for friendship among nations, a friendship that will support the cause of peace for the sake of future generations, this chapter in the history of my country is particularly upsetting.

Javellana's novel tells the story of three gentle-natured cousins who are forced to fight one another as enemies. Two cousins are on the side of the anti-Japanese guerrillas, while the third is a member of the Philippine constabulary who are cooperating with the army of occupation. One scene, in particular, left a deep impression on me. In it, Carding and Gondoy discover that their cousin Polo is among the enemy forces that they are planning to ambush.

> "We have our orders," Carding said quietly. But Gondoy would not be silent. "It is a funny war, this," he sighed, "where one fights against his brother." "Gondoy," said Carding, "Polo is a friend as well as cousin to all of us here. But what is our choice?" "Still it is enough to dampen one's spirit. I wish this war were over."[1]

Through this simple dialogue we feel the poignant struggle to find a right or fair decision regarding the question of violence versus nonviolence.

An Unfulfilled Goal

There is probably no answer to the question of which perspective is in fact "right," and that philosophical ambivalence is what makes this story so tragic. If an approximation to an answer must be given, it would perhaps take the form of a synthesis of these two views in dialectic terms. Thus, the "thesis" of traditional Filipino emphasis on family and blood ties as personified by the gentle Gondoy interacts with the "antithesis" of Carding's strength and hard-headed realism. The synthesis that results from the interaction would represent a leap from a limited, partial view to a larger, holistic perspective. A true sense of fairness must be derived from a universal spirit that is manifested on this higher plane.

In the world of business, such a universal spirit would not be preoccupied with the good of one's own venture or nation. It would always consider the greater, holistic interest of the entire planet and of all humankind, and thereby inspire one to make impartial judgments, even if at times it meant self-sacrifice. That spirit would enable one to transcend personal gain and profit.

In one of the final passages of his famous novel, *El Filibusterismo (The Subversive)* José Rizal states: "I do not mean to say that our freedom must be won at the point of the sword: . . . but I do say that we must win our freedom by deserving it. . . ."[2] Caught though he was in an agonizing conflict between his ideals and reality, Rizal continued to pursue his distant dream of the triumph of nonviolence over violence, of the power of the spirit over brute force. In this sense, a victory of the spirit would also be a triumph of the logic of humanity over the logic of capital.

In the same vein, I believe the February 1986 revolution took the nation a giant step forward toward realizing the dream that Rizal cherished. The fact that an entrenched dictatorship of seventeen years was toppled through the power of the people without recourse to violence is an extraordinary accomplishment that will always shine in the annals of world history.

Dr. Abueva described this victory most powerfully in his inaugural speech as president of the University of the Philippines:

> Our people at EDSA translated into action the greatest virtues of our race—our love of peace and freedom, our sense of community and solidarity, our respect for human dignity, our deeply moral and religious nature. [3]

It was a triumph that signified a momentous and historic advance for the people of the Philippines. Having done that much, each citizen of the Philippines now has a truly precious mission: to move ahead, coming ever closer to the completion of the goals of the revolution that remain unfulfilled. With this thought in mind, I would like to end with a quote from a poem that Rizal wrote in his youth:

> Lift up your radiant brow,
> This day, Youth of my native strand!
> Your abounding talents show
> Resplendently and grand,
> Fair hope of my Motherland!

Soar high, O genius great,
And with noble thoughts fill their minds:
The honor's glorious seat,
May their virgin minds fly and find
More rapidly than the wind.[4]

I hope each of the new graduates of this fine university will achieve personal fulfillment and brilliant success. I am confident that the University of the Philippines will continue in its path of great achievement, contributing to the nation, and to a brighter future for our world.

NOTES

1. Stevan Javellana, *Without Seeing the Dawn* (Boston: Little, Brown and Company, 1947), 284.

2. José Rizal, *El Filibusterismo (The Subversive)*, trans. Leon Ma. Guerrero (Bloomington: Indiana University Press, 1962), 297.

3. Quoted from Dr. José Abueva's inaugural speech, in the official program, *The Investiture of Dr. José V. Abueva as Fifteenth President of the University of the Philippines* (Manila: The University of the Philippines, 1988), 14.

4. José Rizal, *Rizal's Poems* (Manila: National Historical Institute, 1990), 99–100.

The Flight of Creativity

*A speech delivered at the University of Bologna, Italy,
June 1, 1994*

I am truly grateful to be awarded an honorary doctorate by the
University of Bologna, an eminent institution of higher learning
with a long and distinguished history. To Rector Fabio Roversi-
Monaco, let me express my gratitude for the opportunity to speak
today, and I thank all those in the university community gathered
here. I have been asked to share some of my thoughts concerning
the United Nations, and I can think of no place better suited to a
discussion of this topic than the University of Bologna. Throughout
the nine centuries of its history, this university has embodied the
kind of global perspective for which the United Nations stands,
one that transcends the particular interests of its member states.

By the thirteenth and fourteenth centuries, students from all over
Europe flocked here, drawn by the peerless reputation of this university and its community of scholars. They built a cosmopolitan
and independent city. Threatened with aggression by Frederick II,
the students responded, "We are not reeds in the marsh, to be flat-
tened by a single gust of wind. If you come here, you will find us
so."[1] Their lofty and determined spirit is the backbone of global citizenship, then and now.

Supporting the United Nations

As a non-governmental organization (NGO) registered with the United Nations, Soka Gakkai International (SGI) has participated in and supported many UN activities. Since 1982, we have co-sponsored exhibitions in dozens of cities around the world. The themes of three of our exhibits are: "Nuclear Arms: Threat to Our World"; "War and Peace: From a Century of War to a Century of Hope"; and "Toward the Century of Life: The Environment and Development." Their purpose is to call attention to the necessity for all peoples to pool their wisdom in the search for solutions to the global problems that confront us.

Soka Gakkai has also co-sponsored events that bring forward the cause of human rights. In December 1993, an exhibition entitled "Toward a Century of Humanity: An Overview of Human Rights in Today's World" was held at the Palais des Nations in Geneva to commemorate the forty-fifth anniversary of the Universal Declaration of Human Rights. It was displayed there again in February 1994 to coincide with the meeting of the United Nations Commission on Human Rights, and it was then shown in London until the end of May 1994.

The Women's Peace and Culture Conference of Soka Gakkai has also sponsored events highlighting young people around the world. Their exhibits on "Children's Human Rights" and "UNICEF and the World's Children" have been very successful. In addition, the youth of our organization have carried on vigorous campaigns to help refugees. They collected, for example, nearly 300,000 radios that were sent to Cambodia to assist the United Nations Transitional Authority in its efforts to inform the public about the coming general election. I have personally submitted proposals to three UN Special Sessions on Disarmament, and I have offered detailed suggestions on how to attain and preserve world peace as well as viable approaches to the structural reform of the international body.

Soka Gakkai International is not a political organization, nor is it simply a social group. First and foremost, it is a movement that promotes the inner reformation of human beings on the basis of Buddhist philosophy. Accordingly, rather than specific proposals for reform of the United Nations, here I would like to discuss the ideals for which it must strive, the spiritual source of its renewal, and the ethos of global citizenship that will shape its future.

The global system represented by the United Nations is based on cooperation and dialogue. Both are aspects of what I call "soft power," a method whose persuasive strength is spiritual and philosophical. Though there may be times, such as the sad conflict in Bosnia, where the "hard power" of physical force is used as a last resort, the UN primarily attempts to achieve its goals through the application of soft power.

This is, after all, a very young organization; in 1995 it will celebrate the fiftieth anniversary of its founding. In comparison with our long human history, it has barely been born. Considering the brief and struggling existence of its predecessor, the League of Nations, however, the half-century of the United Nations is a major accomplishment.

Increasingly since the end of the Cold War, people are placing their hopes in the United Nations to take a much more active role in assuring world peace. At last the international body is gradually beginning to function as its founders envisioned. It is up to us and to all people of good will to encourage this development, as the United Nations moves into a new century that will be filled with hope.

Cosmic Humanism

Five decades ago, President Franklin D. Roosevelt of the United States was instrumental in bringing the United Nations into existence. Roosevelt inherited the legacy of another American president, Woodrow Wilson, architect of the League of Nations. Like Wilson, FDR had an idealistic, humanitarian vision that encompassed both national and international concerns. His vision became the founding spirit and motivating force of the new world body.

Roosevelt tirelessly persuaded Joseph Stalin, Winston Churchill, and other leaders of the vital importance of global security. FDR's aspirations represented humanism on a grand scale. Some historians have ridiculed them as "cosmic humanism." Certainly, many important UN functions became literally paralyzed during the Cold War. Today, however, people throughout the world are pushing the United Nations to return to its founding spirit, to aim once more for the realization of universal security and world peace. Given these sentiments, humanism on a cosmic scale no longer seems to be a flight of fancy.

As I was considering such issues, I thought of the great Renaissance Man, Leonardo da Vinci. In some ways the parallel may seem strained. Leonardo, in his serene and independent progress through life, seemed to have transcended worldly conventions of good and evil, while the United Nations, by its nature, remains enmeshed in the tortuous wrangling of conflicting national interests.

On the other hand, we need to adopt both a long and short perspective. Karl Jaspers wrote, "Leonardo and Michelangelo are two worlds between which there is little contact: Leonardo a cosmopolitan, Michelangelo a patriot."[2] This observation points up the dimension of Leonardo's outlook that relates to the United Nations, and suggests to us that there has never been a greater need for Leonardo da Vinci's way of looking at the world than there is today.

One lesson we might learn from Leonardo is the importance of self-mastery. Utterly free and independent, he was not only liberated from the strictures of religion and ethics, but was also unconstrained by bonds to nation, family, friends, or acquaintances. He was a citizen of the world, untouchable and unsurpassed. Leonardo was an illegitimate child and remained unmarried throughout his life. Little is known about his family, and his ties to the republic of Florence where he was born were weak. When he had completed his apprenticeship in Florence, he went right off to Milan, where he spent about seventeen years working under the patronage of its duke, Ludovico Sforza. Following Sforza's fall from power, Leonardo spent a short time working for the duke of Romagna, Cesare Borgia. He then moved to Florence, to Rome, and back to Milan as his interests and projects led him. In the last years of his life, he traveled to France at the invitation of Francis I. It was there that he died. Leonardo was not an unemotional person, nor did he lack virtue, but his life is marked by a transcendence of the mundane, and the directed, single-minded pursuit of his calling.

Whatever his circumstance or course of action, Leonardo showed little interest in the divisiveness of contemporary judgments on patriotism, personal allegiance, goodness, beauty, or benefit. Instead, he strove to secure a style of life that would enable him to look upon all things with detachment. He paid no heed to the lures of fame and wealth, yet he was not a rebel against established authority. In his singular devotion to his own affairs, he was impervious to worldly convention.

The Leonardo who created the mysteriously smiling "Mona Lisa" is also the painter of the fiercely fighting, powerful soldiers of the "Battle of Anghiari." The same person who studied hydrodynamics and plant physiology, and who analyzed the flight of birds, also possessed an avid interest in human anatomy. Whatever one can say about Leonardo, the scale of his mind and hands was too grand to be measured by the ordinary norms of society. The freedom with which he rose above worldly concerns provides a glimpse of the truly liberated world citizen. Leonardo's life itself captures the unique freedom and vigor of the Italian Renaissance.

Perhaps what allowed Leonardo to achieve such freedom was his mastery of the self. He himself wrote, "You can have neither a greater nor a lesser dominion than that over yourself."[3] This was his first principle, upon which all others were based. Self-mastery allowed him to respond flexibly to any reality. The conventional virtues of the day, such as loyalty and goodness, were of secondary importance to him. He had no qualms, for example, about accepting Francis I's invitation to go to France, even though this was the king responsible for the downfall of Sforza, his previous patron. Was this a betrayal, a violation of integrity? I see in Leonardo's action, rather, a broad-minded acceptance and generosity of spirit.

Leonardo and Buddhist Philosophy

Leonardo's ability to detach himself from convention reminds us of the Buddhist teaching of "transcending the world" (*shusseken* in Japanese). The "world" refers to the realm of differences, as between good and evil, love and hate, beauty and ugliness, advantage and disadvantage. "Transcending the world" is liberating oneself from attachments to all such distinctions.

The Lotus Sutra, the highest teaching of Buddhism, speaks of the need "to guide living beings and cause them to renounce their attachments."[4] The most profound commentary on this piece of scripture tells us, "The word 'renounce' should be read 'perceive'."[5] It is not enough simply to liberate oneself from attachments; we must also regard them clearly and carefully in order to see them for what they really are. Hence, "transcending the world" means establishing a strong inner self that will enable one to make proper use of any attachments.

Friedrich Nietzsche was another who ignored conventions of good and bad. Speaking of Leonardo, he declared that Leonardo "knew the Orient,"[6] an observation that, I believe, refers to the similarity between Leonardo's spirit and Eastern philosophy. The Sutra and Leonardo are like a highly polished mirror, in the sense that both in some way radiate a spirit that transcends the mundane, and both are able to transmit reality clearly.

The Romance of Leonardo da Vinci, a biography by the Russian writer Dmitry S. Merezhkovsky, contains an unforgettable passage bringing into relief Leonardo's detachment. The artist is standing on a hilltop with his favorite disciple, Francesco Melzi, watching the battle in which the forces of his patron Sforza are defeated by the French army:

> "All that you see here, Francesco, was at one time the bed of an ocean, covering a great part of Europe, Africa and Asia. . . ."
>
> He again looked at the distant cloudlet of smoke, with its sparks of cannon-shots. By now it appeared to him so small in the infinite distance, so tranquil and roseate in the evening sun, whose glow was like that of a holy lamp, that it was hard to believe a combat was raging there, and men were slaughtering one another.
>
> . . . what did it matter which would vanquish the other. . . The fatherland, politics, glory, war, the fall of kingdoms, the uprising of nations—all that seems to men great or awe-

some—does it not, amid the eternal serenity of nature, resemble that cloudlet, melting away in the light of evening?[7]

To one who has attained self-mastery, the reality of war is petty and small. In this description of Leonardo's detachment, Merezhkovsky encapsulates cosmic humanism.

Soka Gakkai International is based on the Buddhist teachings of Nichiren. In our philosophy of human revolution we hear strong echoes of Leonardo's spirit of self-mastery. In order to live our beliefs, we support the United Nations and conduct many other activities for the cause of peace and culture. Through these efforts, we hope to make a contribution to society. At the same time, we strongly emphasize the importance of inner reform in the individual.

As we approach the end of this troubled century, we are surrounded by the tragedy of explosive ethnic conflicts. It seems that the standard modus operandi until now, with its focus on external causes of systems and events, has not served us well. For this reason, I believe we need to cultivate an attitude like Leonardo's that makes self-control the priority if we wish to solve the problems ahead.

No Labor Tires Me

Leonardo dreamed that human beings would someday fly like birds. He, of course, never saw that dream come true, but his own spirit soared in creative flight throughout his life. His extraordinary energy and perseverance is indicated in his writings:

> You will so exert yourself in youth . . . Iron rusts from disuse; stagnant water loses its purity and in cold weather becomes frozen; even so does inaction sap the vigour of the mind . . . Death rather than weariness . . . No labor suffices to tire me . . . [8]

While painting "The Last Supper," Leonardo would sometimes work from dawn to midnight without stopping to eat or drink. For three or four days thereafter he would not touch the painting, pacing the floor, utterly lost in thought. In spite of his amazing concentration, his all-consuming devotion to the act of creation, Leonardo completed relatively few of his works. Most of his paintings, though painstakingly planned and sketched, remained unfinished.

Leonardo was a multi-talented genius of amazing versatility and breadth of interest. In addition to painting, he was a master sculptor, civil engineer, and inventor of myriad devices ranging from flying machines to military weaponry. Most of his work, like his paintings, did not pass the formative stage of ideas and plans and never materialized. It is interesting that he was not at all disturbed by his lack of success in carrying out his plans. He apparently did not regard these incomplete creations as failures or as a source of frustration. He was always curiously unattached to his projects, often moving on to the next before he was through with the current one. Perhaps what seemed incomplete to others was, to him, finished. Otherwise, it would be difficult to reconcile his passion for creation with the enormous number of unfinished works. Perhaps too, his creativity sprang from the synergy between completeness and incompleteness. If so, he personified a complex but meaningful concept: the completeness of incompleteness is simultaneously the incompleteness of completeness.

The spirit of the Renaissance is often described as looking at the whole rather than the part. Leonardo no doubt perceived his world in that way. As Jaspers says: "He considered his work as a totality and held that everything he did must be subordinated to that totality."[9] His creativity—whether in painting, sculpture, invention, architecture, or engineering—was a process in which he called upon his monumental talent in an attempt to incorporate the universal into the particular. In other words, it represented a means of making the invisible world visible. As a result, no matter how perfect a masterpiece he had created, it could not but be incomplete as long as it remained an event in the realm of the particular. We are not meant to rest peacefully in that realm; our destiny is to stay in continuous flight, ever moving forward to the next creation.

The last words of Shakyamuni were: "All phenomena are fleeting. Perfect your practice, never growing negligent." The essential teaching of Mahayana Buddhism also urges: "Strengthen your faith day by day and month after month. Should you slacken even a bit, demons will take advantage."[10] Another passage expresses life's deepest truth:

Even a tarnished mirror will shine like a jewel if it is polished. A mind which presently is clouded by illusions originating from the innate darkness of life is like a tarnished mirror, but once it is polished it will become clear, reflecting the enlightenment of immutable truth.[11]

From the completeness of incompleteness to the incompleteness of completeness—the synergy between these two perspectives is the source of life's infinite creativity, the dynamism of existence.

Reification in Language

Leonardo saw himself as a disciple of experience and sought to observe reality as it is, without preconception. He was, therefore, suspicious of the reifying function of language to capture experience and render it fixed. This emphasis on the visual image and skepticism of the truth of language resembles that of Nagarjuna, the great Mahayana Buddhist thinker of the second or third century.

In his *The Middle Doctrine,* Nagarjuna questioned language, proposing that it tends to reify our experiences and lend substance to that which actually lacks substance. In speaking of the doctrine of dependent origination (*engi,* in Japanese) and the concept of non-substantiality (*ku,* in Japanese), Nagarjuna declared:

The Buddha taught that the nature of dependent origination is not extinguished or produced, it does not exist momentarily or eternally, it is not single or compound, it does not come and does not go; it transcends the vanity of words and is the ultimate bliss.[12]

The reifying nature of language destroys the dynamic synergy of completeness and incompleteness and creates the illusion that a temporary state of stability is eternal. Both Leonardo and Nagarjuna warned that this false security encourages a complacency that seeks the way of least resistance. Leonardo's succinct admonition that "impatience [is] the mother of folly"[13] is especially significant in this context. It also illuminates the danger of radicalism resulting from the confusion of ideals with substance and the consequent haste to implement beliefs, without understanding the nature of either.

Radicalism in politics and society is a major problem today. There is no place for radicalism in efforts to revitalize institutions such as the United Nations. Rising expectations generated by overoptimism about the capability of such organizations to resolve conflicts can easily lead to mistrust when events go even slightly awry. To avoid disappointment, we must remember Leonardo's injunction that "impatience is the mother of folly."

Jacob Burckhardt, a nineteenth-century scholar of Renaissance art and culture, once wrote: "The great man is . . . a man without whom the world would seem to us incomplete."[14] Leonardo da Vinci is such a man, one who illuminates the Italian Renaissance with his genius. Here in the chaos of the end of the twentieth century, we need more people who are as lofty and independent as Leonardo. The creation of a new world order centered on the United Nations will ultimately depend on how many such true cosmopolitans come forth to carry out the task.

The opening of the Charter of the United Nations declares, "We the peoples of the United Nations...." In the search for world peace and stability, it is the people that are most important. Everything ultimately rests with them. For this reason, the United Nations must have the active aid and support of all the citizens of the world if it is to succeed in becoming the parliament of humanity where every voice can be heard.

What is the proof of life? What is the worth of a human being? What is most important in building friendships between nations and among peoples? To address these questions, our dealings with one another must be distinguished by a new commitment to humanism that will support the development of culture and broaden exchange among societies, while recognizing and accepting differences among us. This is the ideal proclaimed in the Magna Carta of European Universities. Institutes of higher learning throughout the world—including Soka University—signed that document on this, the nine-hundredth anniversary of the founding of the University of Bologna. As a Buddhist, I am determined to carry on the legacy of Leonardo. Together, we can succeed in bringing about a new dawn in human history.

In closing, I would like to recite a verse of the great poet Dante Alighieri.

> "You must not be afraid," my leader said,
> "take heart, for we are well along our way;
> do not hold back, push on with all your strength."[15]

NOTES

1. Guido Zaccagnini, *La vita dei maestri e degli scolari nello Studio di Bologna nei secoli XIII e XIV* (Leo S. Olschki, Editeur, Genève, 1926), 7.

2. Karl Jaspers, "Leonardo as Philosopher," in *Three Essays,* trans. Ralph Manheim (New York: Harcourt, Brace & World, 1964), 56.

3. Edward McCurdy, trans., *The Notebooks of Leonardo da Vinci,* (New York: George Braziller, 1958), 1:90.

4. Burton Watson, trans., *The Lotus Sutra* (New York: Columbia University Press, 1993), 24.

5. Nichiko Hori, ed., *Nichiren Daishonin Gosho Zenshu* (Tokyo: Soka Gakkai, 1952), 773.

6. Jaspers, 53.

7. Dmitry S. Merezhkovsky, *The Romance of Leonardo da Vinci,* trans. Bernard Guilbert Guerney (New York: The Heritage Press, 1938), 356.

8. McCurdy, 1:64, 89, 92.

9. Jaspers, 49.

10. Gosho Translation Committee, ed. and trans., *The Major Writings of Nichiren Daishonin* (Tokyo: NSIC, 1980), 1:241.

11. Ibid., 5.

12. Nagarjuna's *Mulamadhyamakakarika* (The Middle Doctrine).

13. McCurdy, 1:83.

14. Jacob Burckhardt, *Reflections on History,* trans. M. D. Hottinger (Indianapolis: Liberty Fund, 1979), 271.

15. Dante Alighieri, *The Divine Comedy,* trans. Mark Musa (New York: Penguin Books, 1985), 2:97.

The Magnificent Cosmos

*A speech given at Moscow M. V. Lomonosov State University,
May 17, 1994*

Nineteen years ago, I spoke at the Culture Palace at Moscow State University on my first visit here. It is a pleasure to have this opportunity once again, as nothing makes me happier than meeting students and sharing ideas with them. I extend my most sincere gratitude to Rector Viktor Sadovnichy and every member of the university who has helped to make this occasion possible.

In January 1994, Moscow State University students spoke out at an informal meeting between the president of the United States, Bill Clinton, and the citizens of Moscow. The occasion was televised in Japan, as perhaps elsewhere. Speaking perfectly fluent English, one student stated that she saw great reserves of spiritual energy in Russia. She went on to express her faith that this nation will become a cultural center of international importance in the near future. It was truly an impressive vote of confidence in the enduring greatness of her country.

The Credo of Mikhail Lomonosov

The founder of Moscow State University, Mikhail Lomonosov, composed these noble lines immediately before his death:

> When our beautiful and spacious land
> Is beset with misfortune
> That is the time
> Russia will give birth to
> Brave and brilliant youth, my progeny
> Following the footsteps of the path I have left.[1]

Two hundred and forty years have passed since this university was founded. During that time, the students and faculty have done their best to live up to the words of its founder. The present members of the university community can be proud of their history. I firmly believe that young people everywhere, like the students at this eminent institution, are the hope of the future, for their countries and the world. As Buddhist scripture tells us: "If you want to understand what results will be manifested in the future, look at the causes that exist in the present."[2]

In 1974, as I prepared to make my first trip to your country, many in Japan questioned my decision. "Why is a Buddhist educator traveling to a nation whose very ideology rejects religion?" they asked. My answer was that I was going "because people are there." Two decades later, in a new, post-ideological world, it is even more important that our focus stay on human beings and the right way to live. As the great contemporary Russian writer Aleksandr Solzhenitsyn so eloquently puts it,

> The structure of the state is secondary to the spirit of human relations. Given human integrity, any honest system is acceptable, but given human rancor and selfishness, even the most sweeping of democracies will become unbearable. If the people themselves lack fairness and honesty, this will come to the surface under any system.[3]

People are the beginning and end of our concerns. Yet, as Tolstoy recognized, they remain the greatest mystery of all. From time immemorial, the question of what it means to be human has engaged the most sustained and profound thought. Yet even after millennia of pondering that question, the answer eludes us. We know that human happiness, for example, cannot be measured in scientific or economic terms alone. Most of us also realize that the great spiritual legacy left to us by the past is perhaps not being used the way it should in present-day society. In the late twentieth century, we seemed to be enshrouded in such dense, dark clouds that any light capable of illuminating the human condition must come from a very bright source indeed.

The Master of Oneself

"Live true to your own life!" was the rallying cry of my mentor Josei Toda, the second president of the Soka Gakkai. He survived two years in prison during the second world war, and he emerged even more firmly undeterred from his dedication to peace. After Japan's defeat, the established values seemed to have been wiped out or turned upside down. In that time of spiritual desolation, Toda preached that the people must return to the very beginning and recreate their own inner human revolution. His teaching brought alive Shakyamuni's observation that we are our own masters, as no one else can ever be; if we discipline ourselves well, we will obtain a master like no other, which in our time can be called human revolution.

Dmitry S. Merezhkovsky, a gifted Russian writer of the late nineteenth and early twentieth centuries, made a similar point when he said: "God has ordained man to be master of himself."[4] These words are repeated three times at the beginning of his book *Peter and Alexis: The Romance of Peter the Great*. The question, "How can one become master of oneself?" flows through the spiritual history of the Russian nation. It seems to me that the people of Russia were more passionately involved with this question in the premodern era than at any other time in history.

The concern for self-mastery is a consistent theme in the life of Peter the Great. It has been almost impossible for historians to reach a consensus about the life of this towering individual. On the one hand, his introduction of Western ideas and technology had the effect of modernizing and developing Russia. On the other, his reforms created a great deal of hardship for the Russian people at the time, particularly as they were brutally enforced by Peter's authoritarian regime. Thus, some historians see Peter as part devil, while others see him as something of a saint. One thing is clear, however; Peter the Great was a giant of a man who dedicated his life to seeking an answer to the broad question of self-mastery.

Aleksandr Pushkin hailed Peter as a ruler of destiny, while the nineteenth-century historian Aleksandr Herzen described him as the first liberated individual in Russian history. Like Atlas supporting the pillars of heaven, Peter bore his own destiny on one shoulder and the destiny of all Russia on the other. Ever since his time, however, his country has been trying to come to terms with the pervasive influence of modern Western civilization. Russia is not the only country that has had to grapple with the complexities of Western influence in society. Usually it is first felt in the military and economic systems, sometimes producing a wholesale transformation of the technology of war. Subsequently, the culture itself may be affected until its very identity is threatened and the people's sense of self is shaken.

The concern for identity appears often in the works of Natsume Soseki, one of modern Japan's most well-loved writers. Soseki attempted to define a Japanese identity during the cultural confusion of wholesale change that occurred after Japan opened its doors to Westernization. Remembering a feeling of impotence in his youth as he observed the chaos around him, he wrote, "I felt as if I had been tied up in a sack, and was unable to escape."[5]

The Decline of Spirituality

Although Japan has changed dramatically in the century since Soseki wrote those words, I doubt that today's Japanese youth are really happy or satisfied with the status quo. It is a mistake to equate happiness with affluence; the joy that material success brings is always transient. Most young people in Japan are alienated and without ambition. Certainly they have more freedom than ever before, but they often lack a clear sense of purpose, and many are confused and uncertain. Some live only for the moment and immediate gratification. Recent polls of high school students around the world indicate that, compared with those in other countries, Japanese students tend to lack hope for the future and to be satisfied with their situation as long as it is comfortable. It seems that, although Japan is enjoying—at least temporarily—unprecedented economic prosperity, its spiritual life has become stagnant. Young people no longer seek to rule their own destiny.

Some individuals, of course, are active, motivated, and directed. Japan still has young people who look beyond their own concerns and have both a sense of purpose and a clear perspective of their own society. There are those who work for world peace, and others who are struggling with essential questions about how human beings should live. These youths, who are conspicuously different from their apathetic peers, continue to give me hope for the emergence of a new philosophy that will lead humanity in the direction of the good, the constructive, and the creative.

How then are we to become our own masters? In the search for an answer to this question, the thoughts of the great philosopher Nikolai Berdyayev may serve as a guide:

> I have never tried, willingly or unwillingly, to shut myself in a private world of my own; rather, I desired to find a way out into the open, to be present in the world and to make the world present within me, but to be present dangerously and freely. Man is created as a microcosmos and his vocation is to recreate the cosmos within himself.[6]

Berdyayev describes the palpable satisfaction felt in achieving self-mastery. That idea, and the evocation of the limitlessly expansive state of being one with the universe, have much in common with Mahayana Buddhist ideas. Mahayana Buddhism posits three stages of transformation in the life of the individual and in the development of the human character. They are: "awakening," "perfect endowment," and "revitalization." I would like to elaborate on these as they relate to the concepts of fundamental order, universality, and self-renewal. I would also like to focus on the strong current of Russian humanism driving toward a higher state of life.

The Fundamental Order of Life

The first stage, awakening, refers to developing an awareness of the fundamental order of life. Buddhism teaches that each of us possesses the Buddha nature, that is, the seed or the potential to develop into an ideal human being. In its essence this nature is adamantine and indestructible, pure and undefiled. When it is revealed, it becomes the core of life which, by enabling us to master ourselves, determines our happiness. In our daily lives, however, the Buddha nature is buried deep under delusions; that is, false, prejudiced, and mistaken views. In order to let the Buddha nature break through and come into full flower, we must push away the many thick layers of delusion. If we can do that, we will awaken to the fundamental order inherent in each of us.

The highest teaching of Mahayana Buddhism, the Lotus Sutra, contains a number of parables intended for those who mistakenly believe that the Buddha is some sort of distant, mythical being, and that they do not possess the Buddha nature themselves. One of the parables tells the story of a poor man who once visited the home of a wealthy friend. As they were talking and enjoying themselves, the poor man drifted off to sleep. His friend, concerned for his welfare, secretly sewed a precious jewel into the lining of his companion's robe while he slept. When the poor man awoke the next morning and said his farewell, he had no idea that a jewel had been sewn into his robe. His life of poverty continued. Several years later, the wealthy man happened to meet his friend again and was astonished to see that he still lived in dire circumstances. When he told him of the jewel sewn inside his robe, the poor man rejoiced.

The jewel is the Buddha nature that we all possess, whether we are aware of it or not. It represents the most fundamental order of human existence, a fulcrum as solid as the one to which the Greek mathematician Archimedes referred when he said: "Give me a firm place to stand, and I will move the earth." To recognize this fundamental order of all being is to gain matchless strength.

The novel *Anna Karenina* is a masterpiece by Leo Tolstoy, one of my favorite authors. Levin, who speaks for the author, is searching for the meaning of life, for the essential nature of existence. In one famous scene, he is enlightened by the words of a peasant:

> One man lives for his own wants and nothing else—take Mityuka, who only thinks of stuffing his belly—but Fokanich is an upright old man. He thinks of his soul. He does not forget God.[7]

These words of an ordinary peasant strike Levin's heart like a bolt of lightning. In this scene, Tolstoy has created one of the most moving and memorable descriptions in world literature of the awakening of one mind by another. How true it is that when one awakens to the fundamental order of the universe—described here as "thinking of the soul"—an entirely new and unexpected world is revealed in all its vigor and glory.

Tolstoy writes frequently of the drama of the conversion from darkness to light and from delusion to awakening. It is roughly depicted in his early works, such as *The Cossacks* (1863), and is more fully developed in the ruminations of Pierre in *War and Peace* and of Levin. The fresh and moving descriptions of this great human emotion that suddenly dawns upon Tolstoy's protagonists reverberate in the hearts of young people everywhere.

Tolstoy was also familiar with the teachings of Buddhism, and the energy of living that he depicted in his writings has much in common with the dynamic view of existence taught in the Lotus Sutra. Both are a paean to the glory of life. We are, after all, "thinking reeds," as Blaise Pascal wrote. The proof of our humanity lies in the construction of our own firm views regarding life, society, and the universe. Happiness is realized when we create our own goals and strive to attain them to the best of our abilities. In this way we will live our lives without any regrets.

The Principle of "Perfect Endowment"

The Buddhist principle of "perfect endowment" ensures that the fundamental order to which we awaken is not partial or prejudiced, but is all-encompassing, equally embracing not only all human beings but nature and the whole universe. It refers to the universality and underlying harmony of life, in a dimension quite different from that of science or reason. The latter are abstract notions; self-contained, impersonal, and structured. In their proper sphere, they exert tremendous power to transform the way we live with amazing speed. Having lived through twentieth-century tragedies of "megadeath," however, we can no longer be sanguine about the unchecked uses of science and reason.

According to Buddhist thought, universality is a symbiotic order in which humanity, nature, and the cosmos coexist, and microcosm and macrocosm are fused in a single living entity. In Buddhism, the idea of symbiosis is conveyed by the term "dependent origination" (*engi,* in Japanese). Whether in human society or the realm of nature, nothing exists in isolation; all phenomena are mutually supportive and related, forming a living cosmos. Once this is understood, then we can establish the proper role of reason.

From this perspective, Levin's sensibility is unique. Lying on his back on the grass and gazing up at the cloudless sky, Levin thinks to himself:

> Do I not know that is infinite space, and not a rounded vault? But however much I screw up my eyes and strain my sight I cannot see it except as round and circumscribed, and in spite of my knowing about infinite space I am incontestably right when I see a firm blue vault, far more right than when I strain my eyes to see beyond it.[8]

Levin is not reverting to primitive astronomy. He is voicing a far-sighted criticism of modernity by a finely honed and subtle spirit. Levin does not perceive the universe to be a bleak realm dominated by pure rationalism. For him, it is full of the vibrance of life, with all the human warmth of joy and comfort, love and devotion, compassion and sympathy.

Tolstoy's emphasis on universality is especially relevant to issues facing the human race today. It poses a challenge to the insularity of extreme ethnic consciousness, which has been one of the major causes of conflict both within and between nations. Levin throws cold water on the self-destructive ethnic passion that made the Serbo-Turkish War seem heroic:

> Yet it's not a question of sacrificing themselves only, but of killing the Turks. The people sacrifice themselves and are always prepared to go on doing so for the good of their souls, but not for the purpose of murder.[9]

Without a universal spirit such as Tolstoy's, we will never see the dawn of a new age of humanism and globalism. The "Russian spirit" of which Dostoyevsky spoke also shares that universality. Both are receptive to humanistic goals, and both reflect the belief that all peoples can and should live in harmony. The pursuit of genuine happiness is in vain unless it is made in this spirit. I believe that life can be truly fulfilling only by working selflessly for the benefit of others. At the same time, inner peace can only be attained by expanding one's consciousness and freeing the "lesser self" from the snares of egotism to awaken the "greater self," which is to be one with the life of the universe as a whole.

Revitalization and Self-renewal

The concept of "revitalization" refers to the cultivation of the creative dynamism of life that allows one to be reborn each day and keeps a person from growing stagnant or rigid. All is change, as the ancient Greek philosopher Heraclitus said. Buddhism also teaches that nothing remains in the same state for even an instant. The hardest stone will eventually be ground to dust; everything must eventually be destroyed. Human society, in particular, is constantly changing. The secret to revitalization is breaking the shell of indolence in which we seek to comfortably rest in the present. Instead, we must listen carefully to the rhythm of change that beats within.

The Buddhist philosophy of Nichiren teaches that "one repeats the eternal cycle of birth and death on the great earth of the state of Buddhahood."[10] By this statement, he means that the power to be continually rejuvenated for all eternity resides within us. Such revitalization is another name for self-renewal.

The self-renewal that Nichiren describes is essential for religious faith. Without it, belief becomes susceptible to dogma. Levin ponders the manifestation of the divine that he feels within himself. He perceives it as supreme happiness and asks:

> Is that happiness restricted to Christians? What about the followers of other religions such as "the Jews, the Mohammedans, the Confucians, the Buddhists. . . ?"[11]

Levin's question is one that must not be sidestepped; otherwise religion will lapse into fanaticism. Doubts of this sort are an expression of an inner power that recreates the self day after day, through the process of self-reflection. They are the source of the humility and generosity of spirit that have been at the core of ethical behavior since ancient times. When religion ignores the process of self-reflection, it risks becoming tyrannical and arrogant, and all too often becomes the rationale for human beings to harm one another.

The fundamental order in the universe provides a foundation on which a person can base his or her life. It promotes inner confidence and serenity. But the outlook it encourages must be kept firm by the sort of continuous introspection that Levin demonstrates, if it is to remain as a vibrant, creative force. From another angle, a perception of universal order that does not generate such ethical values as humility and generosity must be recognized as false and deceptive. Superior human character can be built only when an awareness of fundamental order goes hand-in-hand with a process of self-renewal. For this reason, the stronger you are, the more humble you will be; the more certain you are of your convictions, the more generous you will be.

The true mission of religion is to promote the formation of character and to encourage the quest for self-mastery. That is why Buddhist scriptures place so much importance on self-reflection and urge us to let our inner conscience motivate us. In fact, the main goal of Shakyamuni's life was to cultivate and perfect noble, inwardly-motivated character. It was to this end that his practice was devoted.

Humanistic Competition

As we continue to strive for global unity, educational and cultural exchange that transcends the boundaries of religion, race, and nationality will become ever more important. Since competition, in its constructive sense, spurs progress, I believe that the best way to attain world unity and peace is for nations to compete in what are really character-building activities. Instead of competing to achieve the greatest military strength, for example, countries could vie in the production of strong "global citizens."

The founder and first president of Soka Gakkai, Tsunesaburo Makiguchi, battled Japanese militarism and died in prison at the age of seventy-three. Beginning very early in this century, he insisted that the human race can no longer engage in military, political, or economic competition, but instead must try to foster a climate in which societies compete on humanistic grounds. I hope that the students of Moscow State University will be front-runners in such a humanistic competition of the twenty-first century.

In this discussion, I have referred to Buddhist wisdom and the works of Tolstoy as I sketched the manner in which we can seek to achieve self-mastery. It is up to us to transform chaos into harmony in the coming century, and religion and philosophy, culture and government, all must concentrate on that attempt. I hope all people of similar convictions will join forces with me in our journey down this road to revival.

I would like to close with a beautiful poem from Russia, land of poetry:

> In the open skies, be bold!
> In joy, wake to your mission
> Look! The sun's rays
> Dye the sky golden one moment

And the next are hidden in wisps of cloud
The silver moon drifts
The beauty of spring shoots forth in the meadows
The rosebuds swell
A pure stream flows in the dale
The grapevines shine on the hill
And golden wheat sways in the fields
In stillness, the sighing of the wind's breath
All of this is yours
With joy, pluck the flower of life
Peacefully accept the blessings of heaven
Our world is not a valley of misery
My friend! Be happy
Do not lose your way
Never forget the source of life's daily pleasures
Respect Truth and Law
Do good to others
Then you will leave behind all inconstancy, without fear
And then, in the darkness, you will trust the dawn.[12]

This poem, attributed to Pushkin, assures us that the deeper the darkness, the closer is the dawn. As long as hope exists, happiness will shine. Together with all of you, and with confidence and hope, I look to the dawn of a new civilization.

NOTES

1. M.T. Belyavskii, *In Commemoration of the 275 Anniversary of the Birth of M.V. Lomonosov* (Moscow: Moscow State University, 1986), 109.

2. Gosho Translation Committee, ed. and trans., *The Major Writings of Nichiren Daishonin* (Tokyo: NSIC, 1981), 2:197.

3. Aleksandr Solzhenitsyn, *Rebuilding Russia: Reflections and Tentative Proposals,* trans. Alexis Klimoff (New York: Farrar, Straus and Giroux, 1991), 49.

4. Dmitry S. Merezhkowsky, *Peter and Alexis: The Romance of Peter the Great* (New York and London: G.P. Putnam and Sons, 1905), 11.

5. Natsume Soseki, *Kokoro: A Novel and Selected Essays,* trans. Jay Rubin. (New York: The Pacific Basin Institute, 1992), 294.

6. Nikolai Berdyayev, *Dream and Reality: An Essay in Autobiography,* trans. Katharine Lampert (New York: Collier Books, 1962), 296.

7. Leo Tolstoy, *Anna Karenina,* trans. by Rosemary Edmonds (London: Penguin Books, 1978), 829.

8. Ibid., 835.

9. Ibid., 844.

10. Nichiko Hori, ed., *Nichiren Daishonin Gosho Zenshu.* (Tokyo: Soka Gakkai, 1952), 724.

11. Tolstoy, 851.

12. *The Complete Works of Pushkin in Russian* (Leningrad: Nauka Publishing Company, 1977), 1:389.

PART II

Dimensions
of Culture

A New Road to East–West
Cultural Exchange

A speech delivered at Moscow M. V. Lomonosov State University,
May 27, 1975

Nearly eight months have passed since September 1974 when I last visited Moscow, and I have been eager to see the friends that I made here on my previous visit. When people have talked candidly and become friends, the passage of time cannot alter their feelings for one another. Such friendship transcends whatever cultural or political differences may exist.

Human Will in Russian Literature

In breaking the long bondage imposed by an oppressive social system, the Russian people opened a new chapter in the history of human liberation, and they did it through determination and will.[1] Their indomitable will, which I believe to be the outstanding feature of the Russian national character, has been nurtured and strengthened by the land itself. It is the force that has empowered the people to create a great popular cultural tradition. Russian literature crystallizes the essence of this tradition in the eyes of the world. For me to discuss Russian literature before students and members of the faculty at the Moscow State University may seem presumptuous, but I ask that you take my words as honest reflections of a friend from another country.

The most important characteristic of Russian literature is its concern with what literary pursuits can do to enhance the happiness, freedom, and peace of the people. Literature is not the exclusive domain of a privileged class. It cannot exist without embracing the many people who suffer oppression, hunger, and poverty and who, time and time again, become the victims of war. In many European nations literature has tended to become an artistic end in itself, limited in themes. In contrast, almost all Russian literature reflects keen interest in social problems and a profound concern with the feelings and fate of the common people.

When I read Maxim Gorki's *The Lower Depths* for the first time shortly after the end of World War II, it made an indelible impression on me. In the play, Satin (a character living in a world of decadence and degradation) says, "Man *(chelovek)*! How magnificent! How noble it sounds!"[2] At the time I was at the impressionable age of seventeen or eighteen, living in a nation that had just been defeated in war, a nation that had lost all sense of values. Though we were hungry, my friends and I gathered those few books that had escaped the fires of war and read intensely, searching for a ray of hope for the future. This line from *The Lower Depths* provided that hope, and it has sustained me ever since. In the word *chelovek* I found the characteristic Russian view of humanity, and I felt more sympathetic to Lenin when I later learned that he and Gorki were close friends.

The great Russian writers consistently bring out the enduring hope and faith in the future that the people of Russia have maintained. This hope has been preserved even under unspeakable oppression and conditions of bitter, forced submission. My strong sense of identification with Russian literature derives partly from its concern with the irrepressible will of ordinary people. The organization that I represent, Soka Gakkai, is a social movement whose raison d'etre is the welfare of all people. Soka Gakkai places prime importance on encouraging the shared yearnings of ordinary people to find expression in a spontaneous unity of will, which is the source of energy for peace.

The Russian poet Pushkin, whose status allowed him to write what ordinary people could not put into words, declared that political freedom in his time was inseparable from the liberation of the serfs. Throughout their lives, Gorki, Nekrasov, Turgenev, Tolstoy, Chekhov, and other literary giants were also friends to the common people. No matter how privileged their background or education, they were never able to limit themselves to depictions of the aristocratic way of life. Instead, they invariably produced portraits of human beings in a typically Russian image of humankind. This is true of characters as diverse as Tatyana in Pushkin's *Eugene Onegin* and Platon Karataev in Tolstoy's *War and Peace.*

What did the writers have in mind when they created characters of this kind? I suspect that they were looking beyond the overripe cultures of nineteenth-century Europe to express a hope—even a prayer—for the full flowering and liberation of humanity in our time. Perhaps it was such a vision that so impressed French writer André Gide and other European writers who found in Russian literature something noble and humane.

The Russian concern for humanity is not limited to literature. It also found expression in the uprisings of Stenka Razin (of folk song fame); Pugachev; and in the Dekabristy and Narodniki movements of the nineteenth century. Indeed, the success of the Russian Revolution would have been impossible without an accumulation of energy channelled into human liberation. I would like to believe that the same devotion to the people and their freedom continues to flourish, not only in Soviet literature, but in all other phases of Soviet culture.

Humanity as the Soil of Creative Literature

Once, in a conversation with a young man who, like myself, loves Russian literature, we attempted to think of words that could symbolize different national traits. For the French we selected *esprit* and for the English, "humor." My companion suggested that the word *posledovatel'nost'* would be most apt for Russians. This word means consistency or thoroughness; the refusal to be satisfied until something is completed; a stubborn desire to achieve a goal. This trait undeniably describes the basic nature of Russian literature. As it operates in literature, moreover, it is an idea that, while being very Russian, transcends race, nationality, and language and produces such deeply moving expressions as the word *chelovek* in the Gorki play.

A tradition of this kind cannot be created overnight. In fact, the earliest expression of the *posledovatel'nost'* idea may be traced to ancient oral stories and songs. Few people have as rich a treasury of folk songs, narratives, and proverbs as do the Russians. Most of them come out of the folklore heritage. The story or ballad often tells of a hero who challenges and overcomes evil or peasants rising up against cruel and oppressive landlords. These stories, which are strongly satirical, speak of the soil in which Russian literary traditions are rooted, as well as the powerful spirit of resistance that enabled the people to topple the tsarist regime and repel the armies of Napoleon and Hitler.

A similar spirit enlivens folk songs heard in all parts of the land. Even Japanese know many of these songs. The music of the Cossacks and the famous "Song of the Volga Boatmen" echo more than desperation and the misery of submission. They convey a hope for happiness, even in the midst of their suffering. Both music and lyrics are a protest against unreasonable sorrow. The "Song of the Volga Boatmen," like *Steel* by Ostrovski, is testimony that the deeper the suffering, the greater the spiritual drive to survive the ordeal. Without roots planted deep in the soil provided by the people's love of song, folk tales, and art the literary masterpieces of nineteenth-century Russia could never have developed.

It seems almost natural that the conscientious writers of prerevolutionary Russia were willing to face the suffering of the people squarely. The intense efforts of these men to seek true meaning in literature inspired me to devote my life to the quest for peace and cultural creativity.

A French philosopher once posed this question: "What can literature do to help starving children?" He was questioning the value of literature that demonstrates no concern for social inequalities in a world where human existence itself is threatened. His criticism underscores the narrowness of the literature of Western European nations, for their literary traditions often shut themselves away in enclosed worlds of their own.

Russian literature has developed in concert with the shared longing among the people for happiness, freedom, and peace. It makes questions of the kind asked by the French philosopher superfluous. The profound understanding of human nature reflected in the work of leading Russian writers is firmly rooted in the people themselves. It is they who have nurtured the growth of the national character and ethos. Russian literature could not have been created apart from the people.

In art and other areas of culture, particularism need not conflict with universalism. On the contrary, universal validity may depend precisely on national or ethnic particularity. In times like ours when unity in the world is so urgently needed, the spirit of Russian culture and its deep understanding of humanity must inevitably become an inspirational force for all peoples. This understanding will contribute greatly to the quality of cultural exchange in the twenty-first century, and it is in this area that I believe the young people of Russia will find their mission and responsibility.

Cultural Diffusion Along the Silk Road

The title of this speech, "A New Road to East-West Cultural Exchange," invites comparisons to the Silk Road joining the East and West in the distant past. Winding between two continental regions of oases and steppes, the Silk Road and its many tributaries were a major thoroughfare for trade. Not just objects passed along these routes; they also provided a path for cultural exchange between East and West. Thus, Persian and Scythian culture contributed much to civilizations of later times in other places, while Buddhism fanned out from India to reach almost all of East Asia. Christianity and Islam also colored the art, architecture, music, and ideas of much of the world. All of this exchange was facilitated by the Silk Road. Traveling this route, cultural traditions of Eurasia ultimately reached the Japanese islands.

In the city of Nara, the long-ago capital of Japan, there is a large temple called Todai-ji. Adjacent to its compound is a building called the Shoso-in, which is a repository for a wide variety of objects of immense historical interest dating from twelve to thirteen centuries ago. One of the most unusual is a five-stringed lute decorated with inlaid flowers of amber, tortoise shell, and mother-of-pearl. Boulders and birds flying among the branches of tropical trees are also depicted on this elegant piece. This lute is an eloquent testimonial to the talent, skill, and patience of the artisan who made it.

Four-stringed lutes are said to have originated in Persia. The five-stringed lute, however, arose in India and passed through Central Asia to the Chinese kingdom of the Northern Wei. In China, it is said to have been perfected during the Tang dynasty. The instrument in the Shoso-in is clearly Sassanid Persian in design. Its history, therefore, suggests the manner in which both Persian and Indian cultures traveled along the Silk Road to China, from there crossing the seas to reach Japan. The Silk Road thus precipitated the blending of different cultural elements and stimulated the development of new cultures.

In addition to the lute, the Shoso-in houses among its many treasures a harp from Mesopotamia, a decorated wooden box from Egypt, and glass from the Eastern Roman empire. Although these articles were the exclusive property of the ruling class and tell us little about the intermixing of popular cultures, they are an example of the manner in which cultural exchange—even if only for the privileged—took place in the past.

What was the reason for the wide cultural diffusion that took place along the Silk Road? Certainly, trade and conquest are two causes of dissemination of cultural traits, but I believe a more important one lies in the very nature of culture as an instrument of exchange. Culture is essentially universal; it is the breath that enlivens the activities of human life. Joy strikes a sympathetic chord in the hearts of all people and causes harmonious reverberations. Similarly, culture is a fundamental human undertaking that conquers distance and stirs the hearts of peoples everywhere. I believe that this sympathy among human hearts is the point of departure for cultural exchange and the basis of culture itself.

The fundamental nature of culture is accord and harmony. It is diametrically opposed to force, especially the force of arms. While military power threatens humanity and imposes control from without, culture arises from within the human mind as a liberating force. Furthermore, the logic of power assumes that militarily and economically strong nations will conquer smaller and weaker ones. By contrast, cultural exchange requires the positive acceptance of another's viewpoint; the autonomy of the recipient is a necessary condition. Finally, military power is geared toward destruction, whereas culture is premised on creativity.

Thus, culture represents an enduring product of human life and rests on a framework of harmony, autonomy, and creativity. The flowering of culture is the one way to liberation and resistance against military might and political power. I am convinced that Russian literature suggests the path that will lead to cultural growth in the future.

The Silk Road was instrumental in promoting East-West cultural interchange and cultural development in the lands of Central Asia. Nevertheless, the route was gradually abandoned after the eighth century, following the rise of the Saracen empire and the ravages committed by the Mongols in the oasis cities along the way. The destructive influence of military power on cultural endeavors can be awesome. It is sometimes argued that military expeditions stimulate cultural contacts and diffusion, but, as we all know well, armed force can be deadly to culture. War in the modern age can devastate or destroy culture; worse, it has the potential to obliterate civilization itself.

As the continental Silk Road became more difficult to travel, Europeans sought a sea route to the Far East. Assisted by scientific developments, the Portuguese and Spanish succeeded in opening routes eastward around the Cape of Good Hope at the tip of Africa. Thus the overland route across Central Asia lost its practical value, and the Silk Road, which had been a priceless connection between East and West, fell into disuse.

Uniting Human Hearts

In the twentieth century, advances in the technology of transport and communications have made it possible to travel from one place to another at great speeds. An incident that occurs in a remote country may be known in all corners of the globe by the end of the day. Technology has increased the volume of exchange between East and West to a level unimaginable in the heyday of the Silk Road. Nevertheless, I am always startled to realize how vast are the distances that still separate human hearts even while improved transportation is shrinking the world. Although efficient transmission of information and commodity transactions take place on a large scale, interactions on the personal, human level among the peoples of the world remain limited.

Individuals with a global view of the human condition agree that the best way to unite the hearts and minds of all people is through cultural networking on the broadest possible basis. In my travels I have heard people everywhere speak of their desire for East-West cultural interchange. At no time in history has there been as great a need for a spiritual Silk Road extending all over the globe, transcending national and ideological barriers, and binding together peoples at the most basic level. Cultural interactions that are a spontaneous manifestation of the popular will can turn suspicion into trust, convert hostility into understanding, and lead the world away from strife toward lasting peace. Too often history has witnessed the overnight dissolution of agreements made solely on the governmental level. The tragic wars that political failures have brought must not be repeated.

There are those who sincerely believe in the historical reality of national or ethnic hostilities. Such antagonisms do persist, but they are essentially based on delusion. Recently, I read the interesting autobiography of Melina Mercuri, an internationally famous Greek actress who from childhood had considered the Turks to be enemies. When she traveled to Nicosia, on the island of Cyprus, to work on location for a film, she found the city divided into hostile Turkish and Greek quarters separated by checkpoints that she, however, was permitted to cross. She was frequently entrusted with messages or small gifts from Greeks to Turks on the other side of the boundary. As time passed, Turkish people, also, started asking her to perform similar errands and to take letters and other things to their friends in the Greek zone. Reflecting on this experience, Mercuri said to herself, "These two groups can be friends. Governments find it convenient to stir up hostility between them; but if they were left to themselves, the Turks and the Greeks could live together in peace."

Although it may seem difficult to break away from conditions determined in history, people living today have absolutely no responsibility to burden themselves with the animosities of their forebears. When one person recognizes the humanity of another, walls that may have been separating them crumble. I am speaking with everyone here at this moment; we are engaging in an exchange grounded in our friendship and shared desire for peace.

I am convinced that even difficult, apparently insoluble problems can be resolved peacefully, without recourse to arms, if they are worked out on the human level. No person, however powerful, has the right to inflame one group against another or to cause the shedding of human blood. Let me say again that the word *chelovek,* as it is employed in Gorki's story, must be sublimated in a cry of peace and the unification of all humankind. To unite this world and to build lasting peace, I proclaim the pressing need for a spiritual Silk Road which will join the hearts of the peoples of East and West.

In all practicality, how should we promote exchange? Our world is divided into the so-called advanced industrialized nations, on the one hand, and a large number of nations at various stages of development, on the other. One of the most important issues of the day is to find ways to stimulate fruitful relationships between these two groups. Economists and political scientists describe the issue as the "North-South problem," referring to the disparities between the "have" nations of the North and the "have-not" nations of the South. Each country, of course, regards the situation from its own point of view.

I have spoken above of East-West relations. This does not refer to relations between communist and capitalist countries, but rather exchanges between Western and non-Western cultures. In discussing the North-South issue as well, I am not examining social systems. We must not confuse political or economic systems and cultural heritage. Unless this distinction is clear, there is a danger that the basic nature of the cultures involved could be misunderstood and fruitful exchange impeded.

The distinction between the "have" North and the "have-not" South is based entirely on the level of economic development. Successful industrialization, however, does not prove the value of a culture. On the contrary, economically developing countries all have cultures as rich and complex as nations who outstrip them in wealth and power. It is desirable to use standards other than economics in evaluating the achievements of a people. For example, what would we find if we examined the nations of the world in terms of musical achievements? In terms of non-economic aspects of human culture, "developed" nations might appear much less advanced than others that are now regarded as "developing." We would possess a more varied and accurate picture of our green planet and its four billion people if it were examined in the light of the art, religion, traditions, lifestyles, and psychology of its inhabitants. The present distinction between advanced and developing nations would become meaningless. Today the relationships between the nations of the North and South do not deserve the designation "exchange." Too often, they are unilateral, so dominated by the North that they are criticized as economic or cultural aggression.

A Spiritual Silk Road Encircling the Globe

Cultural exchange can bring people together everywhere. Exchange can be like the string of a lute striking harmonious vibrations in the hearts of all. There can be no such harmony, however, without a steadfast mutual recognition of equality. Unilateral cultural intrusions plant the dangerous seed of pride in the transmitter and fill the hearts of the recipients with feelings of inferiority or hatred. Genuine exchange can take place only when people approach each other with an honest sense of equality, mutual respect, and appreciation of other cultures. When everyone sees the world this way, we will have built a new spiritual Silk Road that joins East and West, North and South, in a spirit of trust and respect.

The Soviet Union provides an instructive example of how to build bridges spanning the cultures of East and West and how to stimulate fruitful exchange between North and South. This is due in part to the distinctive and profound Soviet interpretation of human nature. Geography also plays a part, having put the Soviet Union at a crossroads between East and West. The Soviet experiment in bringing together fifteen different republics, all at various levels of economic development, into a single nation, represents one more valuable example of cultural exchange between North and South. Indeed, the 126 peoples of the Soviet Union, which include Russians, Ukrainians, and many Asian peoples, make this nation a great melting pot in which different cultures and races have been harmonized without sacrificing their identity.

The Soviet Union today is nothing like tsarist Russia. Under the tsars, the ruling elite encouraged discord among groups for the sake of political expediency. In contrast, one of the first measures taken by the Soviet government after the revolution was to proclaim equal rights for all peoples of the union, regardless of ethnic identity or economic level. When the Soviet Union was founded, Lenin said that he hoped for a federation of nations based on free will, complete trust, and a strong sense of brotherhood. Even in the nineteenth century, the peoples of Russia were already aware of the need to bridge Eastern and Western cultural spheres. Under the tsars, the scholarly study of Eastern cultures was highly advanced. Soon after the revolution, the complete works of the Indian poet Rabindranath Tagore were translated into Russian. Indeed, the historical opposition between Westernizers and Slavophiles may have begun in the recognition of possible East-West unity. Thus, the Soviet Union is in a unique position to understand the sensitivities of both Asia and Europe, and of the developed North and the developing South. For that reason also it has a great mission to promote cultural exchange.

I expect great things to come out of the desire for peace of the Soviet people. They have cultivated an undying spirit of resistance against oppression over the years. It helped Russians endure two centuries of destruction and conquest by Mongolian tribes beginning in the 1200s, and it fortified them to turn back invasions by the Teutonic knights, Swedes, and the armies of Napoleon. Finally, it gave them the strength to survive the ravages brought about by the armies of Hitler. The spirit of resistance has implanted a pure longing for peace in the hearts of the people of the Soviet Union.

I place my hopes in the Soviet people to bear the responsibility for creating a spiritual Silk Road connecting the minds and hearts of the peoples of the world. I feel certain that they will draw fully on their long, pacific tradition in their efforts to bring about lasting peace. Speaking for myself, and for Soka Gakkai, I promise that we will do our best to encourage cultural exchange on the non-governmental level. I will devote the rest of my life to the promotion of such exchange, and I am certain that our joint efforts will bring us together again someday.

NOTES

1. In 1975, when this speech was written, Russia was still part of the Soviet Union. We have retained the author's several references to Russian people and literature, however, to preserve his historical emphasis on the background and ideas in literature that energized Soviet culture as a whole.—Eds.

2. Maxim Gorki, *The Lower Depths,* trans. Alex Szogyi (New York: Samuel French, Inc., 1964), 63.

The Mexican Poetic Spirit

From a speech delivered at the University of Guadalajara,
March 5, 1981

In my capacity as founder of Soka University and president of Soka Gakkai International, an organization dedicated to peace, culture, and education based on true Buddhism, I have traveled widely. Yet this is my first visit to Mexico in sixteen years. It is a great pleasure to be here again. I hope that in some small way my visit will contribute to increased exchange between Mexico and Japan in the realms of culture, education, and the peace movement. Today, the last day of my visit, I should like to thank Dr. Enrique Zambrano Valle, rector of Guadalajara University, for giving me this opportunity to speak. And I am grateful to the members of the faculty and student body who have gathered here to share some of my thoughts on the poetic spirit of Mexico.

Historical Ties

Relations between Mexico and Japan are by no means of recent origin. In the early years of the seventeenth century, a powerful feudal lord of Japan, Date Masamune dispatched a retainer, Hasekura Tsunenaga, on a mission to Spain and Rome. On the way to Europe, his party passed through Mexico, which was then under Spanish rule. In *Samurai,* a recent novel by Shusaku Endo, the hero is modeled on Hasekura. The book itself has provoked much discussion, and, eager to see how it portrayed Mexico at that time, I read it with great interest.

In 1888, several decades after Japan emerged from two and one-half centuries of seclusion, the government signed a trade treaty with Mexico. This was the first treaty in modern times between Japan and a foreign nation that was premised on the equality of the signatories. In the years since the end of World War II, our bilateral relations have become very close politically and economically, as well as in education and culture. The development of mutual understanding on the people-to-people level, as opposed to governmental level, however, is still just beginning. I am determined to do everything I can to help our citizens know each other better.

In 1980, the International Congress for the Study of Asian Peace was held in Yokohama, Japan. Many distinguished people from Asia and elsewhere attended, among them the Vienna-born scholar Ivan Illich, director of the International Cultural Information Center of Mexico. While his rejection of conventional schooling and some other of his ideas were a little difficult to accept, he offered powerful insights that impressed me strongly. Among the several statements by Illich that appeared in the Japanese press, one was, "My concern is that people should be poetic, that they should tell jokes and learn to smile."

This seems a disarmingly naive remark, yet it can teach us much. The poetic spirit and a smiling face are the most telling indications that the pathways linking the minds and hearts of people are open and functioning. We can talk about peace and cultural exchange ad infinitum, but it is almost meaningless unless there is true communication that touches the inner chord in each individual. A famous passage in the UNESCO Constitution says as much: "War is born in the hearts of humankind. Therefore we must build fortresses of peace within the heart."

Why does Illich underscore the poetic spirit and a smiling face? There are doubtless many reasons, but a principal one perhaps relates to his knowledge of and experience in Mexico, where he has lived since 1960. Although my knowledge of Mexican history and culture is limited, I have formed a clear mental picture of the temperament of the Mexican people; a temperament marked by smiling faces, poetic spirits, and by a special kind of warmth. I am certain that my image of Mexico as the "land of sunshine and passion" is not merely a superficial impression. I believe that their love of fiestas, for example, stems from the determination of the Mexican people to enjoy whatever life may bring. No matter what trials they are called upon to face, they will never abandon their essential gentleness and cheerfulness, or the courage underlying those qualities.

Value of a Smile

This brings to mind an episode recounted in *Insurgent Mexico,* a vivid piece of reporting by the American journalist John Reed. In 1923, government forces and revolutionaries were engaged in armed hostilities, making a complex situation even more chaotic. Undaunted, Reed set off for Mexico. Near the southern border of the United States, he encountered waves of refugees fleeing the fighting in Mexico and seeking safe haven in the United States. The border guards were inspecting them for weapons, examining both men and women with a roughness and a thoroughness far greater than the circumstances warranted.

Reed reported that as he was standing at the river crossing he saw a woman holding up her skirts and wading across the shallow water. She was wrapped in a heavy shawl, which seemed to be hiding something that bulged out suspiciously in the front.

"Hey, there!" shouted a customs man. "What have you got under your shawl?"

She slowly opened the front of her shawl, and answered placidly: "I don't know, señor. It may be a girl, or it may be a boy."[1] In such tense and frightening circumstances, this woman's banter revealed a firmness of nerve that would put many men to shame.

A second episode connected with the Mexican Revolution concerns Pancho Villa, who is remembered with respect and affection by the local people. In March of 1913, the strategic area of Torreon was under attack by the revolutionary forces. Villa and the men under his command had reached Yermo, to the north, and preparations had been completed for an attack on Torreon itself. Suddenly everyone noticed that Villa was nowhere to be found. His officers waited impatiently for four days, until at last he appeared, tired and muddy. He explained that, having promised to attend a friend's wedding, he had slipped away from the encampment. For the past four days and nights he had been feasting and dancing to celebrate the nuptials.

I smiled when I first read this anecdote. It seemed to convey so vividly the personality of this romantic, courageous man; he refused to let the rules of military discipline dominate his rich human feeling and personal loyalty. Though the incident speaks of Villa's personality, it also illustrates something about the nature of the Mexican people. The same quality is evident in the action of the woman at the river crossing. Both incidents are redolent with the national character I clumsily described as "smiling faces, poetic spirits, and a special kind of warmth."

There is nothing mawkish or sentimental in the Mexican character. The Mexican Revolution, like so many other revolutions, was won through struggle and sacrifice by the people of the nation and was paid for in their blood. It is said that even women took up arms and went into battle. Doubtless there are many tragic stories about those struggles. Yet, these two episodes symbolize the way the people held fast to their intense love of life, even during painful periods of suffering. It is precisely this sensitivity to human feelings and values that lies behind the respect for human rights and the dedication to freedom, equality, and independence that Mexicans demonstrate today.

In 1967, the treaty banning nuclear weapons from Latin America was drawn up, and an international organization to be known as OPANAL was established in Mexico City to implement the treaty provisions. I understand that these steps were taken as a result of a strong Mexican initiative. This action, which goes much further than the nuclear non-proliferation treaty, was taken in a positive spirit of independence characteristic of the Mexican people.

Human Values First

Nuclear arms constitute a more frightful, devastating type of weaponry than has ever been known before; no greater outrage against the spirit of humanity can be imagined. Recourse to such weaponry could actually lead to the destruction of all humankind. That is why I take every opportunity to call for a total ban on and the abolition of nuclear arms. One proposal that merits consideration is the establishment of nuclear-free zones. It could be carried out under the aegis of the United Nations, and the zones could eventually be enlarged until the world is free of these terrible weapons. I am especially grateful for the continuing efforts of the Mexican people to create such a nuclear-free zone in Latin America.

Their efforts reflect Mexico's long-held concern for human rights and values and its determination to establish the kind of society that will allow men and women to live as human beings should. It is the same concern that led the Mexican people to give warm support to the Popular Front in its struggle against fascism at the time of the Spanish Civil War.

The full realization of freedom, equality, and independence is a difficult task. Modern Mexican history might be described as moving through a process of trial and error, marked by frequent setbacks and frustrations. Many political, economic, and other kinds of problems remain to be solved. Nevertheless, I believe that the men and women of Mexico are capable of great acts in the future. The soul of the Mexican people, never faltering during three hundred long years of colonial oppression, has been fortified and tempered by the experience of revolution and independence. I am convinced that this country will make contributions to humanity that will parallel the artistic achievements of the Mexican Renaissance masters Rivera, Orozco, Siqueiros, and Tamayo.

A painter friend of mine who knows Mexico well tells me that when welcoming a guest, it is customary to say, "My house is your house, too." This is a wonderfully warm and friendly greeting, and it conveys the temper of the country very well. Buddhist scripture contains a parable that has a similar meaning. Long ago, in India, there was a tradition of binding twenty or thirty long, slender reeds together into a bundle. The story, called the "parable of the two reeds," was first employed by Shariputra, a disciple of the Buddha, who was famous for his unparalleled wisdom.

"Let us suppose that there are two bundles of reeds," Shariputra said. "As long as the two are leaning against each other, they stand up. In the same way, because there is a 'this,' there can be a 'that,' and because there is a 'that,' there can be a 'this.' But, if we take away one of the bundles of reeds, the other will fall over. In the same way, if we take away 'this,' 'that' cannot continue to exist; and if we take away 'that,' 'this' cannot exist."

Here we have a lesson in interdependence: people cannot exist in isolation; they depend upon each other for help. The Mexican greeting to welcome guests—"My house is your house, too"—embodies the same wise understanding of human interdependence.

With the rising tide of internationalism, a more lively degree of cultural exchange will engage more and more countries. The time has come when nations must meet one another on the basis of complete equality and mutual benefit. To achieve that, we need ongoing dialogue that will link the hearts and minds of all peoples. I sincerely hope that my visit to Mexico will help, even a little, to speed the realization of that goal.

In closing, I would like to address a few words particularly to the young people and students of Mexico. Each of you will soon be called on to employ your knowledge and fervor in facing the challenges of the twenty-first century. I sincerely hope that not only will you become worthy leaders of your country, but that each of you will be a responsible and dedicated supporter of the cause of world peace.

NOTE

1. John Reed, *Insurgent Mexico* (New York & London: D. Appleton and Company, 1914), 4–5.

A Harmonious Blend of Cultures

*A speech delivered at Saint Kliment Ohridsky University
of Sofia, Bulgaria,
May 21, 1981*

At the kind invitation of the Government of Bulgaria, I am at last here, on Bulgarian soil. I am very grateful to Sofia University for awarding me an honorary degree. I thank Rector Ilcho Dimitrov and others who gave me the opportunity to speak, and all the professors and students who have taken the time to attend my lecture today.

Before coming to Bulgaria, I spent some time in the Soviet Union, where I met with Premier Nikolai A. Tikhonov. I strongly emphasized to him the importance of cultural exchange as the best way for one people truly to know the heart of another. To this end, Soka University and Moscow State University are engaged in an ongoing program of educational exchange, under which students and professors from each institution visit the other. While I was in the Soviet capital, the Ginrei Chorus, made up of students from Soka University, performed at Moscow State University as part of a Japan-Soviet Student Friendship Festival. The mingled voices of the Ginrei Chorus and the Science Academy Chorus from Moscow State University seemed to erase all boundaries of nation, language, and culture.

It is my understanding that choral singing is very popular in Bulgaria and has achieved high standards recognized throughout the world. I have heard, in fact, that your country is known as "a king-dom of choruses." In the past, three Bulgarian choral groups (the Men's Chamber Choir of Bulgarian Radio and Television, Tolbuhin Children's Choir, and Svetoslav Obretenov Bulgarian Capella Choir) have visited Japan under the sponsorship of the Min-On Concert Association, which happens to be one of the projects I most enjoyed setting up. They performed a total of one hundred seven-teen times throughout Japan and left a strong impression on their audiences. The Bulgarian folk songs especially touched the hearts of the listeners. I am eager to expand and perpetuate this type of spiri-tual rainbow that bridges the hearts of different peoples.

Youthful Culture Within a Distinguished History

It is toward that end that I have spoken with two of Bulgaria's ambassadors to Japan and Bulgarian Minister of Culture, Lyudmila Zhivkova. Our discussions have deepened my understanding of this country, whose culture is not as well known in Japan as it should be. In 1975, when I met Ambassador Serbesov for the first time in Tokyo, I remember telling him that I thought Bulgaria seemed to be a very young country, and that the image of the rising sun aptly symbolizes its future. That feeling has been reinforced each time I come across another cultural achievement of Bulgaria.

Ivan Minchov Vazov's *Under the Yoke,* widely regarded as a master-piece, has been translated into thirty-two languages. Since reading this thought-provoking example of Bulgarian literature, I have become even more keenly aware of the youthfulness of the Bulgarian people. This book deals with the April Revolt of 1876, when the Bulgarian population rose up valiantly in an attempt to free themselves from the domination of the Ottoman empire. The vivid portrayals of steadfast human love reminded me of Victor Hugo's *Les Misérables,* which was among my favorite books in my youth. It is well known that Hugo was among the dedicated intellectuals who strenuously protested the Ottoman government's cruel suppression of the April Revolt.

Although the revolt failed, Vazov's protagonist, Ogunyanov, says: "It is sad, but it is not shameful." This statement is full of pride and courage, virtues that typify youth and characterize the hearts of all

*Delivering the speech "Creative Life" at the Institut de France
(June 1989)*

"The Age of Soft Power" is well received at Harvard University
(September 1991)

At the invitation of the Gandhi Smriti and Darshan Samiti, Mr. Ikeda speaks on "Gandhism and the Modern World" (National Museum of India, February 1992)

Speaking on "The Kemalist Revolution: A Model" at Ankara University (June 1992)

Under the auspices of the Chinese Academy of Sciences, Mr. Ikeda gives his speech "An Ethos of Symbiosis" at the Chinese Academy of Social Sciences (October 1992)

President Austregésilo Athayde of the Brazilian Academy of Letters introduces Mr. Ikeda as a newly appointed non-resident member of the academy, where he will speak on "A Garden of Imagination" (February 1993)

*At the invitation of Moscow State University, Mr. Ikeda gives the lecture
"The Magnificent Cosmos" (May 1994)*

Affirming mutual commitment to human rights issues together with Rosa Parks, mother of the American civil rights movement (Los Angeles, January 1993)

Talking with Dr. Linus Pauling, Nobel laureate in both chemistry and peace, confirming their belief in a world without wars, the need to support the UN, and hopes for the world's youth (Los Angeles, February 1987)

*Conferring with United Nations Secretary-General Boutros-Ghali
(Tokyo, December 1993)*

*President José V. Abueva of the University of the Philippines and Mr. Ikeda unveil a
plaque engraved with the name Ikeda Hall at the university's Deliman campus
(Manila, May 1993)*

Soka University in Tokyo, opened in 1971, is dedicated to becoming a fortress for peace.

the people of Bulgaria. Vazov himself says that even if the revolt should be branded reckless or criticized by historians,

> Poetry alone would have shown it forgiveness and crowned it with a hero's laurels . . . for the sake of the rapture which sent those meek Anatolian tailors onto the heights of Sredna Gora. . . . It was a poetic madness. For young peoples, like the young, are poets.[1]

I see Bulgaria as a young culture, but I recognize that it has its own history and traditions, which may be the oldest within Slavic civilization. In the ninth and tenth centuries during the reign of King Simeon, the first Bulgarian empire blossomed into one of the most prosperous cultures in the contemporary world. The vestiges of the second Bulgarian empire, which emerged at the end of the twelfth century, may still be found in the old city of Turnovo. Throughout its thirteen-hundred-year history, this glorious tradition has maintained tremendous energy, like the magma of a volcano. Unfortunately, for five hundred years Bulgaria was held down through what we call the dark ages, governed by the Ottoman Turks. It was a bitter period, but the spirit of Bulgaria never died. Within the depths of the Bulgarian soul the spirit of the people remained steadfast. When, in the nineteenth century, Bulgaria experienced its great Renaissance, it was like the spectacular eruption of a long-quiet volcano.

It seems especially significant that geographically, historically, and spiritually Bulgaria has often found itself at a crossroads between East and West. Here the two traditions fused while at the same time confronting and clashing with each other. That valuable experience may move the Balkan peninsula into an important role in constructing a new human society based on a union of East and West.

Intimacy Between God and Humans

It may seem easy to discuss the possible blending of Eastern and Western cultures, but it is a vast subject with many complex and diverse aspects. To focus on just one aspect, I will take up the nature and role of the Eastern Orthodox church, an institution with deep roots in the history of Bulgaria.

I myself am a Buddhist and my religious tenets differ considerably from Eastern Orthodoxy. To me, the strict monotheism of Christianity, whether Eastern or Western, is its salient feature. In the eyes of Christians, perhaps the main feature of Buddhism is its basis in the Law (dharma) rather than a god, and, consequently, its atheistic appearance. Instead of speaking of doctrine, therefore, I would like to examine how the Bulgarian Orthodox church helped to preserve the spirit of the people and supported their freedom and independence, a contribution that I believe is very significant.

In the past, Eastern Orthodoxy has experienced stress from both inside and outside. The church was pressed hard by the Greek Orthodox church after it gave way to the authority of the Ottoman empire. A symbol of courage during this period was the work of Brother Paisii, a monk who wrote *The History of Bulgarian Kings, Biographies of Saints,* and other volumes toward the end of the eighteenth century. Father Paisii, who would become known as the "father of Bulgarian culture," and other members of the church devoted their lives to protecting the cultural integrity of a people dominated for five centuries by the Turks. Their achievements were hailed during a ceremony to commemorate the thousandth anniversary of the establishment of Rila Monastery. During this celebration, Georgi Dimitrov stated that the Orthodox church should be honored for its great historic undertaking of protecting the Bulgarians' national consciousness and their lives.

Religion has played a major role in determining the course of history. It is my impression that the relationship between God and people seems much closer within the Eastern Orthodox church than in Roman Catholicism, for example. When God is close to human beings, numerous intermediaries are not necessary. Of course, as long as a religion postulates only a single deity, there will always be a clear distinction between God and humanity, but the Roman Catholic ecclesiastical hierarchy increases the distance between God and individual Catholics. As the embodiment of church authority, the pope, also, is separated from the people by his

immensely elevated status. I understand that ecclesiastical intermediaries are fewer in number within the Eastern Orthodox church.

When distance is created between God and humans, there
emerges a disparity between the clergy and laity and between
divine and secular power, also. Much of the history of the Middle
Ages and modern times in Western Europe is dotted with a succession of conflicts between religious and secular authorities. A sense
of division remains even today between politics and religion.

Jean-Jacques Rousseau, who was considered something of a
heretic in his own society, once wrote:

> However, since princes and civil laws have always existed, the
> consequence of this dual power has been an endless conflict of
> jurisdiction, which has made any kind of good polity impossi-
> ble in Christian states, where men have never known whether
> they ought to obey the civil ruler or the priest.[2]

Even though it shares the same Christian roots, the world of
Eastern Orthodoxy developed differently from that of Roman
Catholicism. With that in mind, I would like to examine interpretations of the theory of the divine right of kings. When it empowered secular authority to subjugate religious authority, it worked to
negative effect, leading to the misuse of religion by the political
hierarchy. Arnold J. Toynbee called this practice the "idolization of
an institution" and suggested that herein lay the primary reason for
the short lifespan of the Byzantine empire. On the other hand, the
idea of divine right looked at in a broad sense can be credited with
creating an intimacy between politics and religion that can be
constructive.

In the Roman Catholic world, the choice was always either "politics for the sake of religion" or "religion for the sake of politics." I
strongly believe that politics and religion should commit themselves
to a common concern: nothing less than the well-being of humanity. Needless to say, both spheres can best fulfill their original roles
only when they uncompromisingly maintain total dedication to
human welfare rather than to their own interests. Realization of

this possibility seems more likely where there is an ongoing effort to bridge the gap between God and human beings, clergy and laity, and divine and secular powers as in Eastern Orthodoxy.

In the past, this possibility was not fulfilled, and both the Greek and Russian Orthodox churches made unfortunate compromises, as in their complicity, to one degree or another, with the dictates of the Ottoman rulers. In my view, because Eastern Orthodoxy has been harshly tested over a long period in Bulgaria, if there is any chance for the strengths of the religion to flower, then perhaps it exists in Bulgaria.

A Humanistic View of God

I would like to draw a parallel with Leo Tolstoy's view of religion. As you may know, he was excommunicated as a heretic from the Russian Orthodox church. Toward the latter part of his life, he asserted that "the country of God is within yourself."[3] He also wrote, "God can be perceived only within ourselves. Unless you discover God within yourself, you will discover God nowhere."[4] In Tolstoy's perspective God and human beings can hardly be separated. How reminiscent of Tolstoy, therefore, are the words in the poem "A Prayer," written by Khristo Botev (1848–76), a revolutionary poet of Bulgaria. Botev wrote:

> O, my God, Thou Lord of Justice
> Not the one in far off heaven
> But thou, God, who dwell'st within me,
> In my heart and in my doing."[5]

It is less strange than it may seem to compare Botev, a revolutionary poet who took up arms and died young, with Tolstoy, an old man of literature who martyred himself for his philosophy of love, urging, "Do not protest against evil." Both were the cries of two souls deeply rooted in the soil of Slavic and Balkan traditions. Though different in form, the humanitarian love expressed by these two writers in no way opposes the ideal of socialistic humanism that your country values so much. It is a kind of love that one can find an echo of in the Buddhist view of the human being—the view that Buddhahood is immanent within the life of each individual.

In this sense, it is meaningless to discuss the God cherished by Tolstoy or Botev merely in terms of religious doctrine. The point that each was trying to make at the risk of his life was that everything, including religion, exists "for the human being." Both insisted that if this is forgotten, any doctrine or ideology swiftly descends the slippery slope to moral decadence.

In referring to the April Revolt of 1876, Ivan Vazov said, "The national spirit of Bulgaria has never been raised to such height, nor is it likely to rise again."[6] I believe that the national spirit of Bulgaria soared during the April Revolt because it was fired by the compulsion to protect the dignity of human beings at any cost.

The future of Bulgaria's national spirit depends upon the wise judgment of its citizens. As long as the banner of humanity proudly waves over Bulgaria, barriers between nations will surely be transcended, opening the way toward a global humanistic society in the twenty-first century. I believe that this society will be like a vast lush field where Eastern and Western cultures will blend, and the flowers of peace and culture will bloom.

I have heard that the lion is the symbol of Bulgaria. The lion possesses deep meaning within Buddhism. King Ashoka of ancient India, whose peaceful rule was based upon the spirit of Buddhism, constructed a pillar at the top of which were four lions looking out over Sarnath, near Benares. That is where Shakyamuni Buddha expounded the Law for the first time, for the sake of the happiness of all people. Thus, the lions atop the pillar symbolize the voice of Shakyamuni. His teachings were penetrating like the lion's roar, overpowering all other voices to move people's hearts. The same spirit possessed Nichiren Daishonin, whose teaching became a system of Buddhist thought. As I travel through the world as a believer in Nichiren's teachings, I never stop hoping that his voice will be heard. Let me conclude with a prayer that Bulgaria will forever wave the banner of human liberty, peace, and dignity, dauntlessly and bravely like a lion king.

NOTES

1. Ivan Vazov, *Under the Yoke,* trans. Marguerite Alexieva and Theodora Atanassova, ed. Marco Mincoff (Sofia: Foreign Languages Press, 1960), 438.

2. Jean-Jacques Rousseau, *The Social Contract,* trans. Maurice Cranston (London: Penguin Books, Ltd., 1968), 179.

3. Leo Tolstoy, *Jinsei no Michi,* trans. Kyuichiro Hara (Tokyo: Iwanami Shoten, Ltd., 1939), 1:37.

4. Ibid., 37.

5. Khristo Botev, *A Prayer, The History of Modern Bulgarian Literature,* trans. Clarence A. Manning & Roman Smal-Stocki (New York: Bookman Associates, 1960), 176.

6. Vazov, 343.

Crossroads of Civilization

A speech delivered at the University of Bucharest, Romania,
June 7, 1983

I have been invited to speak at many universities in many parts of the world, but this is the first time that I have visited Romania, a beautiful country graced with luxuriant flowers and trees. On a visit to the Village and Folk Art Museum in Bucharest, I was delighted to meet several young boys and girls who are being raised with the beauty and strength of mind needed to ensure a bright future for their country. As I watched the children performing folk dances in the museum plaza, they seemed to be reminding us that without sunlight, freedom, and peace, the future of the world is dark indeed.

The soul of the Romanian people shines through the dancing children. It will be up to them, and others like them, to realize the immense possibilities that Romania can bring to the new century. The promise of Romania is also encapsulated in its national emblem, a brilliant sun rising in the distance behind oil derricks and mountains clad in venerable, ancient trees.

Historical Drama

Romania is well known in Japan, not only for its abundant natural resources and rapid economic growth, but also for its rich treasure trove of folklore. Music is an important part of this tradition. During the summer of 1981, people came from all over Japan to hear three Romanian musicians when they participated in a series of concerts called "A Musical Voyage Along the Silk Road." Their tour was sponsored by the Min-On Concert Association, which I founded. The audiences were especially charmed by the lighthearted sound of the folk instrument called the *nay*. Its sounds seemed to echo the joy and sorrow in the soul of the Romanian people, for among those echoes I sensed tones of the country's turbulent past.

Called Dacia in ancient times, what is now Romania was conquered by the Roman empire and invaded by Goths and Huns. The area was incorporated into the Byzantine cultural sphere at the same time that the Slavs were moving southward, and it was eventually governed by the Ottoman Turks. After centuries of trials and struggle, Romania began moving toward independence in the latter half of the nineteenth century. Throughout this vast historical drama, the Romanian people may have felt that their hearts were locked beneath the frozen ground, but they never gave up their striving for freedom and independence.

Herodotus wrote of the Dacians as being the bravest and most just of all the people of Thrace. Later, even though Dacia came under the influence of Roman culture, its people were neither enslaved nor subjected. Instead, they intermarried with Romans, producing a blend of Dacian and Roman civilizations that greatly strengthened the rich Romanian culture. This historical background is reflected in the independent foreign policy Romania pursues at the present time.

Throughout the centuries, many different cultures have mixed into and deepened the spiritual soil of Romania. Certainly the fusion of distinct cultural traditions has added to its treasure trove of folklore. I find it especially significant, however, that Romania has been influenced by three great civilizations: Christian Europe, Byzantium, and Islam. Historically and geographically, Romania is located at a major juncture of civilizations.

Contact between different cultures has often been accompanied by conflict, invasion, and sometimes conquest. In many cases, these clashes have ended in the apparent obliteration of a culture. But sometimes these cultures have persisted in the hearts of the people, running deeply like an underground stream. Transformed over time, they burst forth again into the light when the time is right. Endurance is made possible by the inherent power of cultural traditions.

A Precarious Balance

In East Asia, we have a saying that an understanding of the new can only be achieved by study of the old. Thus, new vistas of the future will open only to people who respect and care for their cultural heritage. From that vantage point, as we contemplate the coming century, the critical importance of finding an optimal balance between the part—individual societies and cultures—and the whole seems self-evident. But let me explain this point further.

A series of scientific discoveries and technological developments beginning in the fifteenth century, which opened the Age of Exploration and brought about the Industrial Revolution, have drastically reduced the space that once separated peoples and civilizations. Today it is considered natural that societies are linked together into a global system. It is no longer possible to view world economics solely from the standpoint of any one nation. The oil crises of the last decade, for example, were a vivid demonstration of the interdependence of the world's economies. Present-day technology, moreover, allows instant, global transmission of information, creating a greater sense of familiarity among nations. It was satellite broadcasting that brought the triumphs of Romania's Nadia Comaneci into many Japanese living rooms during the Montreal and Moscow Olympic Games.

Much more ominous and immediate, today's interdependence involves everyone in the mistakes and failures of others, as well as the successes. I speak of the threat of nuclear war. If the Soviet Union and the United States should launch their missiles, there would be no victor and no vanquished because all humanity would be teetering on the precipice of annihilation. Nuclear weapons have galvanized the whole world into a single community sharing a single fate. It is patently clear that for better or for worse, we must think of the entire world as unified in some fashion. Otherwise, we will find ourselves incapable of taking any action. We are being prodded toward unity, but the road ahead will not be an easy one.

Think of the folly being played out right now. There are forty armed conflicts taking place somewhere in the world with the direct or indirect participation of forty-five nations. The sheer numbers are awful enough, but these conflicts are all the more horrifying when you consider that human beings with weapons can be more brutal than any other creature on earth.

To bring the nations of the world together, the great obstacles created by conflict must be overcome. That cannot be accomplished without the relentless efforts of organizations like the United Nations committed to justice, peace, and human welfare.

The Whole and Its Parts

Although nations and states constitute individual entities, they are not necessarily what I mean by "parts" of the whole. While we must respect them in accordance with the "Five Principles of Peace," they are basically artificial units whose boundaries are political by nature. As such, they represent the product of modern nationalism, which first took shape in Western Europe a few centuries ago. Behind the concept of nation-state, however, lies infinitely varied human culture resting on thousands of years of history and tradition. Culture is passed from generation to generation in distinctive local forms stored in the hearts of people. As their folklore reveals, Romanians have their own distinctive culture, just as Japanese have theirs.

The Swiss philosopher Verner Kaegi used to talk about a unified world, warning us that no matter what form that unity assumes, the world will survive only as long as the cells within it are strong and healthy. The cell is like the village of old that nurtured its people, letting them prosper and lead spiritually fulfilling lives. Kaegi's concept of the cell seems analogous to discrete cultures, whether based on ethnic groups or some other affinity. It is the "part" as opposed to the "whole." Each separate part must be respected for itself if we ever hope to realize the ideal of a unified world. It is vital to achieve that unity without violating the integrity of the individual parts and to maintain a proper balance between the two. The difficulty of this task is starkly illustrated by the dilemmas many nations are currently experiencing as they attempt to modernize with the help of science and technology. Frequently, they must sacrifice the traditional, which is to say that the smaller "parts" feel stress as they are pressured to achieve modernization—another word for global unification.

Let us imagine a boat being rowed across a lake, and let us equate the boat with traditional culture and the oars with modernization. No matter how stout the craft or how vigorously the oars are pulled, no progress can be made if the waters of the lake are turbulent. The essential ingredient needed at this time is placid water, that is, peace. Calming the waters requires us all to accept a set of universal spiritual values that bind individual, local, and cultural traditions, while still allowing each to shine on its own. This requires a worldwide spiritual transformation, without which humankind will be unable to cope with the advance of modernization and the development of technology.

At this point, I would like to recall the words of Mircea Eliade, who was born in Romania and became one of the greatest religious philosophers of this century. Eliade hoped that the encounter between the peoples of the modern West and the non-Western world would bring forth a new humanism. Only someone born and bred at a crossroads of civilization could have coined the simple expression "new humanism," with its wealth of possibilities for the future. As of the present, however, Eliade's vision has yet to be realized in any clear form. Some sensitive people have almost given up in despair. Madame Alva Myrdal, Swedish winner of the 1982 Nobel Peace Prize, has stated frankly that people are increasingly unwilling to listen to pleas for peace, and that even she is beginning to grow weary of the struggle. I believe that we must focus on the deep currents of history and not on superficial events. How do we discern those undercurrents? If we listen carefully to the people, and gently knock on the door of their hearts, I believe we will hear the sounds of movements deep inside that foretell peace.

The Pacifist Spirit

In the depths of their hearts, ordinary people everywhere are truly cosmopolitan and devoted to peace, and perceptive writers of genius have often depicted them so. One such writer is the Bulgarian novelist Zaharia Stançu. His masterpiece *Barefoot* revolves around the understanding and friendship existing between Romanians and Bulgarians during a time when the latter country was at war with Turkey.

The setting of the book is a village located just across the Danube from Bulgaria where Bulgarians regularly come to sell seeds in spring and vegetables in autumn. The frequent contact has given rise to a warm and earthy friendship between the two peoples. Suddenly, war with the Turks breaks out, and the Bulgarians stop coming to the village. Before long, word comes that old familiar friends such as Ivan and Stoian have fallen in the field of battle. Worse, a militiaman comes to the village to conscript Romanians, who will then be forced to fight their old friends. The description of how the villagers muttered among themselves when they heard this shocking news creates a vivid, unforgettable scene:

> War against the Bulgarians? What have we against the Bulgarians? We were friends. A good thing Ivan and Stoian are dead. We'd have met them. What a shame it would have been! We'd have fought and shot one another. Dear God, dear God![1]

As this despairing, heartfelt outburst powerfully shows, the villagers may have been uneducated, but their very lack of learning has kept them free of prejudice and animosity. Firmly rooted in the earth of human life, they give us a picture of human souls that are lifted high above considerations of race or nationality. This is not intended as praise of ignorance, but a reminder that learning and knowledge, no matter how great, derive their value only from service to the people.

All truly great literature must have both universal appeal and the ability to portray the hearts and minds of a people in fine, sensitive strokes. Stançu's work qualifies on both counts, illustrating as it does the cosmopolitan outlook and pacifism of ordinary people.

Spontaneous Sympathy

I remember hearing about an incident that occurred in Japan about the same time as the events depicted in Stancu's book: it brought out qualities in Japanese that were strikingly similar to the characters in *Barefoot*. In 1904, at the beginning of the Russo-Japanese war, Japanese troops captured a Russian officer and an enlisted man and took them to their regimental headquarters. The first Russian prisoners to be taken, these men were something of a curiosity for the Japanese soldiers. When a company leader asked who wanted to take a look at the Russians, only about half the men raised their hands. The leader asked the others why they did not want to go, and one enlisted man spoke out for all: "Back in my home village, I was a craftsman. When I put on a uniform, I became a fighter for my country, a Japanese *bushi*. These men are our enemy. I don't know what kind of people they are, but they are also fighters for their country. I think it is too bad that, now they've been unlucky enough to be captured, they have to be dragged around here and there and made a spectacle of. I feel very sorry for them and don't want to embarrass them by gawking at them."

The commanding officer was impressed by this opinion. Gradually, the other men came to see things the same way, and the trip to look at the prisoners was called off.

For me, this episode is an uplifting example of human sympathy expressed in the midst of war. The anonymous former craftsman had no desire to participate in war. Rather, he took pride in his own work, which he considered worthy of high respect. By refusing to abandon his dignity as a human being, even when he was forced to go into battle, he swayed the thinking of other men. I sense a certain regret in his remark that he does not know what kind of people the prisoners are. No doubt, this Japanese soldier imagined that the Russians also had families and jobs somewhere in their own land. His reaction, like that of the villagers in *Barefoot,* expresses the down-to-earth sympathy characteristic of ordinary people everywhere.

The notion of shame plays a prominent role in both episodes. The Romanians considered it shameful to fight against their Bulgarian friends. The Japanese soldier did not wish to embarrass the Russian prisoners by gaping at them. This common feeling seems to tell us that human minds can converge in harmony and understanding, regardless of the distances and differences that seem to separate them.

An old saying has it that the answers to the most remote questions are to be found at one's own front door. In other words, we must appeal to the feelings that are common to us all if we are to generate the new humanism I referred to earlier. In my opinion, the natural sympathy and understanding of people everywhere must be the soil in which the new humanism can thrive. Ideologies and slogans will not help, but when universal understanding and sympathy have calmed the waters of our lake, the boat of tradition and the oars of modernization—the whole and the parts—can advance together toward the twenty-first century.

The flow of history pauses for nothing, and the task of creating the new humanism rests on all our shoulders. As a believer in Nichiren Daishonin's Buddhism, which teaches the dignity of humanity, I will continue to devote myself to the fulfillment of that task. I hope that everyone will join me in working hand-in-hand for a new century, when a splendid unified world will prosper, both materially and spiritually.

NOTE

1. Zaharia Stancu, *Barefoot,* trans. and ed. Frank Kirk (New York: Twayne Publishers, Inc., 1971), 266.

A New Global Awareness

A speech delivered at the University of Macau,
January 30, 1991

I would like to express my gratitude to Dr. Jorge A. H. Rangel, president of the Macau Foundation, to Dr. Hsueh Shou Sheng, rector of the University of East Asia,[1] and to the many members of the distinguished faculty. I am honored to be here, and especially grateful to be the recipient of the first honorary professorship conferred by the University of East Asia.

The Open Window of Macau

Starting in the sixteenth century, Macau was an entrepot for the Portuguese trade with China and Japan, and it has played a crucial role in connecting East and West ever since. Macau has also served as a transit port for Sino-Japanese trade and provided a window through which Japan and other peoples gained much of their early contact with European civilization. On this first visit to Macau, I have been deeply impressed by the scenic beauty of the island. Traditional Chinese structures blend with typical Portuguese-style buildings. The city is living proof that the cultures of East Asia and Europe can coexist in harmony.

95

In 1990, Dr. Rangel delivered a lecture at Soka University in Japan. He made the point that for four and one-half centuries Macau has shown the world that the fusion of Eastern and Western cultures is possible. In this age of globalization, I believe that Macau will be recognized for the example it provides of cultural coexistence and for the precedent it sets as we seek harmony among all peoples.

About to celebrate the tenth anniversary of its founding, the University of East Asia mirrors the international character of Macau. The faculty includes distinguished scholars from China, the United Kingdom, Portugal, France, the United States, Canada, Germany, Australia, New Zealand, and Japan. The university has established an agreement for academic exchange with Soka University and is vigorously promoting similar exchanges with many other universities and research institutions throughout the world.

In 1981, a total of one hundred thirty-five rectors and chancellors from colleges and universities in twenty-six countries attended the opening ceremonies for the University of East Asia. This is testimony, first, to the firm determination of the faculty, administration, and student body to play a leading role in the international age, and second, to the great expectations that educational institutions in other countries have for the university. I share these expectations, and believe that the University of East Asia will be an important influence in bringing about an "age without borders" in this part of the world. This institution promises to be like the sun, rising in hope from the land of Macau to brighten the twenty-first century.

The Gulf War presents a grave crisis to a world where there is still no new system to replace the bipolar domination of the United States and Soviet Union. A fresh approach that would open the way for the spiritual unification of humankind is not in sight. Instead, all we see is chaos. The collapse of ideology has led to an explosion of nationalistic passions. Most agree that nationality and ethnicity are important in establishing particular identities, but neither by itself offers a way to start building a new global order. Norman Cousins once asserted that the primary mission of education lies in teaching people not to be "tribe-conscious" but to be "human-conscious" in their thinking. The tribalism innate to all of us at some subconscious level must be replaced—through education, philosophy and religion—by a more open and universal consciousness directed toward humanity as a whole. Lacking this consciousness, new mechanisms for maintaining global stability will never materialize.

In considering this challenge, I am reminded of the sense of order and harmony flowing like an underground stream through three thousand years of Chinese civilization. The same spiritual current underlies the Confucian five cardinal virtues—benevolence, justice, propriety, wisdom, and sincerity—which are the motto and founding ethos of the University of East Asia. In recent years, the remarkable pace of economic development in Japan and the newly industrialized economies (NIES) of East Asia, which include South Korea, Taiwan, and Hong Kong, has become the focus of world attention. Economic success, in turn, has sparked interest in the religions, thought, and other aspects of Asian cultures. These countries and territories, along with mainland China, have been described as constituting an "Asian cultural sphere" or "Chinese-ideograph culture sphere." Clearly, the significance of Asian culture transcends economics and should be considered from the perspective of the history of civilization.

Individualism and Liberalism

About ten years ago, the prominent American Sinologist William Theodore de Bary of Columbia University published a collection of lectures originally delivered at the Chinese University of Hong Kong, entitled *The Liberal Tradition in China*. In this book, he analyzes such central concepts of Chinese culture as self-motivated learning, self-control, upholding propriety, assuming personal moral responsibility, and self-attainment. In conclusion, de Bary argues that the Neo-Confucianism of the twelfth-century philosopher Zhu Zi, while generally considered to form the ideological basis for feudalism, actually contains elements that correspond, at least in part, to modern European individualism and liberalism.

All the Neo-Confucian concepts de Bary discusses focus on the individual "self"; their basic theme is the logical connection between personal enlightenment and liberty. In this philosophy, individual autonomy is based on self-restraint. For example, the notion of pursuing learning because you want to, for your own sake, is predicated upon self-awareness. It contrasts with forced learning, such as the knowledge students pursued under the classical examination system in China. The attainment of knowledge for its own sake, as Dr. Rangel has said, is indeed introspective and self-reflective.

Although de Bary does not mention it, there is something very Cartesian about the concept of the autonomous, introspective individual. Descartes lived and worked at a time of philosophical chaos brought on by the collapse of medieval scholasticism. His famous, meaning-laden maxim, "I think, therefore I am" (*cogito ergo sum*) was the product of an exhaustive process of self-examination. It crystallized an essential insight that became the foundation for the structure on which his entire philosophy was subsequently built. The figure of Descartes, master of himself, striding gallantly down his chosen path, is an imposing one and justifies his renown as the father of modern European philosophy.

It is important to note, however, that while Cartesian philosophy can be used to validate the untrammeled autonomy of the individual, it is almost entirely devoid of reference to an "other." On this point it diverges sharply from the concept of individualism or liberalism expressed in Chinese philosophy.

In the Chinese injunction to attain self-mastery and observe "propriety," for example, the introspective "self" is clearly involved with the "other" through the medium of social ritual, which defines acceptable, correct behavior. Thus, the liberal currents in Chinese thought differ from those in Europe, in that the existence of society as the organic nexus for the life and activities of the individual is always assumed. In this respect, traditional Chinese thought exhibits a down-to-earth sense of harmony, which might be defined as the acceptance of responsibility for the betterment of society and the conditions of human existence. In this connection, de Bary states:

Here a radical individualism would seem to be ruled out, and what I would call a Confucian personalism takes its place—a concept of the person as most truly itself when most fully in communion with other selves.[2]

Clearly, the term "a radical individualism" refers to the European perspective, whose innate limitations have become increasingly apparent as society has developed.

The contrast between Western-style and Chinese individualism has generated serious interest from scholars who are studying the rise of Northeast Asian cultures. For example, the erudite Leon Vandermeersch, a leading French Sinologist, states that his goal was to expose the detrimental tendencies of Western "ultra-individualism" and to encourage greater self-awareness and self-examination among Western people.[3]

We cannot, of course, deny or underestimate the great historical significance and achievements of European individualism. Our contemporary notion of human rights, for example, is forever indebted to the ideas developed in the Declaration of the Rights of Man and the Citizen. This document was written two hundred years ago in France in the interest of protecting the dignity of people from the intrusions of a powerful state authority. The Declaration, in turn, was based on the spirit of individualism as understood at the time. I must concede that in Japan, awareness of human rights lags behind that of the West.

That said, I see the central defect of Western-style radical or ultra-individualism in pitting the naked and vulnerable human being against the state. Further, the rights of each person are given such strong emphasis that they destabilize and threaten the organic social setting where human activities unfold. As the French Revolution illustrates, placing excessive emphasis on the confrontation between the state and the individual tends to eliminate the small and medium-scale communities that exist between the two poles.

Although the same tendency often occurs in societies where state authority has expanded and become centralized, it is actually quite rare for the individual and the state to come into direct confrontation. People spend most of their time in smaller-scale surroundings—at home, at the workplace, or in the local community. These settings are where our face-to-face, immediate engagement with others takes place. Our self-discovery occurs in these surroundings, because it is here that we most acutely sense the reality of our existence and appreciate the joys of life and living.

When a person living in an unstable communal framework is forced into direct confrontation with the state, he or she is likely either to experience anomie or to become susceptible to totalitarianism. We have seen this happen time and again during the present century.

The Five Cardinal Virtues

There is a well-known anecdote about the legendary sage-king Emperor Yao, which is startling in the contrast it poses to the kind of political leadership we are used to today. The story describes the common people living in an idyllic state of peace and contentment. One day, concerned about the efficacy of his rule in bringing happiness to his people, Emperor Yao disguises himself as a commoner and ventures into town. At the edge of the town, he comes upon a grey-haired old farmer who, while patting his belly and spinning a wooden top, is singing a song:

> I rise with the sun to work
> And rest when it sets.
> For water, I dig a well.
> To eat, I plow the fields.
> What is the power of an emperor to me?

This story contains a wonderfully sound and cheerful affirmation of life and captures the spirit that gave birth to and fostered the great Chinese tradition of individualism. Having long been obscured by other historical currents, this aspect of Chinese thought has been unearthed by Western scholars. The question of why this tradition, which contained the germ of many liberal elements, failed to come to full fruition merits much more study.

But the fact is that this spiritual heritage is present and is beginning to be recognized. The sense that harmony characterizes the normal, right state of affairs permeates three thousand years of China's history; it might be described as an "innate awareness" of the Chinese people, a sensitivity that brings order to the human spirit and gives it a cosmopolitan outlook. Such a unique spirituality is clearly manifested in both Chinese Buddhism and the Mahayana Buddhism of Japan as the all-embracing and intensely affirmative "perfect teaching" (*engyo* in Japanese). This dimension of Chinese thought provided de Bary and Vandermeersch with hope for a way out of the deadlock in which European-led civilization now seems trapped.

Sun Yat-sen, who spent part of his youth in Macau, wrote that proper morals are essential to permanently sustain the well-being of the people and the nation. He was speaking of a morality that cannot be attained through formalistic practice of courtesy and ritual. It must be developed by cultivating the outlook that I have called "innate awareness," the belief in a larger order or harmony. Similarly, the Five Cardinal Virtues that are the motto of the University of East Asia—benevolence, justice, propriety, wisdom, and sincerity—will be given new life and find new meaning as guidelines for the twenty-first century when interpreted in the light of this great Chinese tradition.

These five virtues are the subject of much discussion in Buddhism, and I would like to take a Buddhist perspective in considering their significance to contemporary living. Benevolence, the first, suggests an awakening of humanism and humanitarian action. More broadly, it implies the kind of love which is directed to the whole of humanity.

The second, justice, begins with the conquest of egotistical impulses. The world is now in a time of transition. While the sovereignty of nations must be respected, excessive and parochial nationalism needs to be overcome. We must strive to affirm the primacy of humanity as a whole and act for the benefit of the entire human family. The prerequisite for becoming a world citizen is precisely to conquer egotistical urges.

The third cardinal virtue, propriety, refers to acknowledging and respecting the existence of others. Our world is an aggregation of many different peoples and countries, each with its own culture and mores that help define and identify it. The peaceful coexistence of nations is based on accepting, understanding, and respecting these cultural differences.

The fourth virtue, wisdom, is the source of all creative endeavor. Wisdom could help us deal fairly and constructively with such disasters as the war in the Persian Gulf, which has not only cost many lives but has also precipitated environmental contamination on an appalling scale. Such events threaten us and our world, but to resolve them, we need to free ourselves from rigid modes of thinking. Opening ourselves to different possibilities will give us access to fresh sources of wisdom that can bring a flexible and adaptive approach to solving the problems of the world.

The last of the five cardinal virtues is sincerity, but it also has the meaning of fidelity. It is the basic quality needed to transform distrust into trust, hostility into understanding, and change hatred into compassion. The elements of confidence and friendship cannot be cultivated "strategically." Without genuine trust, the people of the world will never be able to open their hearts and minds to one another.

Zhou Enlai and Wen Tianxiang

One individual who artlessly and naturally manifested these virtues was the late premier of China, Zhou Enlai. I had the privilege of meeting him on my second visit to China in December 1974, about a year before he passed away. I have also been honored by the continued friendship of his widow, Madame Deng Yingchao. Our meeting took place in a plainly-furnished hospital room in Beijing where Premier Zhou was recuperating from an illness. Despite his infirmity, he insisted on rising and coming to the door to greet me and to say goodbye. Noting the sparse furnishings of his room, he frankly acknowledged that "China today is not affluent."

He discussed the prospects for friendship between peoples, friendship based on a spirit of equality and mutual benefit that would continue for generations to come. During our discussion, he revealed an appealing humility combined with a harmonious sense of balance and self-restraint. These characteristics were coupled with a powerful willingness to discipline his life according to his convictions, and a self-control that was instantly apparent by his speech and demeanor.

Another who had the courage to live his life according to his convictions was Wen Tianxiang, who lived in the thirteenth century, during the Southern Song dynasty. One of his most famous poems described the expanse of sea surrounding Macau. After passing the examinations for government service with honors, Wen became a general of great intelligence and valor. He was captured while resisting the invasion of Mongol (Yuan) forces. The Mongols, admiring his ability and character, attempted to win him over and persuade him to change sides in the war. He wrote a poem at that time that goes something like:

When I was defeated by the Yuan
at the edge of the rapids of Huangkong in Jiangxi,
I was filled with panic and dread.
I lamented my solitude on the Sea of Lingding.
Since ancient times has there ever been anyone who escaped
death? If I am to die,
then I would at least want to leave to the world
a record of loyalty and sincerity,
which will shine in history.

With this poem, Wen Tianxiang expressed his refusal to change loyalties, fully knowing that it would mean his death. Eventually he was executed, but his name continues to shine as an example of a magnificent hero who lived by his convictions until the last moment of his life. Wen Tianxiang's story moves us even today, because it illustrates aspects of humanity that are truly universal, with meaning that transcends the specific circumstances of his life and death.

Here in Macau, Sun Yat-sen dedicated himself to the reform of feudal China. This is a place for inspiration, a setting in which youth can awaken to their ideals and goals in life. I envision the students here at the University of East Asia as the pioneers of a new spirit, carrying a truly humane consciousness from this "harbor of new global wisdom" out across the great ocean of a peaceful twenty-first century.

NOTES

1. The University of Macau was founded in 1981 as the Universidade de la Asia Oriental. The name was changed to the University of Macau in 1991, after Mr. Ikeda's speech.

2. Wm. Theodore de Bary, *The Liberal Tradition in China* (New York: Columbia University Press, 1983), 27.

3. Leon Vandermeersch, *Le nouveau monde Sinise* (The New Chinese World) (Paris: Presses Universitaires de France, 1986), *passim*.

The Making of History

A speech delivered at Fudan University, Shanghai,
June 9, 1984

A few days ago at Beijing University, I spoke of the strong inclination in Chinese civilization and culture to value literary and artistic accomplishments over those associated with martial ideals. I noted how this tendency has acted to restrain the nation from engagement in warfare and military activities. In an attempt to trace the origins of that tendency in China's traditional ways of thought, I touched on aspects of China's intellectual history. Today, I should like to focus on the Chinese view of history with regard to questions about human life and its meaning.

A Mirror and Source of Light

Few countries can rival China in the depth of its concern for history. India, for example, exhibits a relative lack of interest in the subject. Chinese, in comparison, have been almost fanatical in their efforts to observe and record historical events. The voluminous literature that has resulted is aptly described by the colorful phrase *hanniu chongdong,* meaning books so numerous that they "make the oxen transporting them sweat, and fill the house they are stored in to the rafters."

Over the centuries, the Chinese people have honored two proverbs: "Study the old in order to understand the new," and "borrow antiquity to explain the present." Together they express the traditional belief that history is a mirror reflecting the present; it is a beacon illuminating our time.

Although I know little about what view of history prevails in China at present, certainly since the Chinese Revolution all fields have tended to concentrate on the role of the common people. The late Chairman Mao stated that "The people, the people alone, are the motive power that creates history." That comment articulates a view of history that places the common people and their interests at center stage. Such a perspective represents a clear break with the traditional Confucian-inspired view of history, which focused upon the role of the ruler, and whose highest ideals were embodied by Yao, Shun, and the other mythical sage-rulers of antiquity.

No matter how one judges the Confucian view of history, it is deeply embedded in several thousand years of Chinese tradition. It cannot easily be uprooted. No doubt this is why the modern writer Lü Xun (who regarded such historical consciousness as a kind of cannibalism) thought it was important for people to undergo a revolution in their thinking. Although he recognized that it may be difficult to achieve, Lu Xun believed that people had to free themselves from the old ways of thought.

Traditionally, history was deeply respected; historical experience was perceived as a mirror and a source of light that clarifies the present and guides the future. I believe that this positive heritage is very much alive in China today. For example, Chinese often employ quotations from the classical literature in their speeches and writings. History seems to hold powerful meaning and to be a living reality in the present. The Chinese view of history is very different from that which has prevailed in Europe since the eighteenth century. In Europe the influence of nineteenth-century historicism in particular magnified the differences between the two. To be sure, historicism made its own contribution by emphasizing objectivity and the need to support statements and theories with facts. A more important effect of this approach, however, has been the objectification of history itself. In one school of historiography, history has come to be thought of as subject to laws of its own, and its dynamic interactions with human beings have been severed.

Solidarity of World Citizenry

Friedrich Nietzsche, who so clearly foresaw the crises of modern European civilization, said:

> We employ history for the sake of life and action; we do not use it for some easy secession from life and action, and we certainly do not employ it to dress up or disguise a life that is self-centered or actions that are cowardly or base.[1]

I think we can replace the word "life" with "human being" in this statement. Throughout his life Nietzsche struggled against the subversion of values in views of history that took no account of the people, the main force in historical development. In contrast, Chinese traditionally regarded history as assisting in the creation of a better today and tomorrow, as food for life and human beings. The Chinese perception of history is perhaps best symbolized in the work of the ancient historian Sima Qian (Ssu-ma Chien). Rather than viewing history as a cold, impersonal process subject to laws of its own, Sima Qian and others approached it with passionate subjectivity and moral concern; theirs was a quest for instruction in how human beings ought best to live.

In a famous passage from his voluminous works, Sima Qian comments upon the relationship between literature and human suffering. It is a passage that never fails to move and inspire courage in me:

> Of old, when the Chief of the West, King Wen, was imprisoned at Youli, he spent his time expanding the *Book of Changes;* Confucius was in distress between Chen and Cai and he made the *Spring and Autumn Annals;* when Qu Yuan was exiled, he composed his poem "Encountering Sorrow"; after Zuo Qui lost his sight, he composed the *Narratives from the States;* when

Sunzi had his feet amputated, he set forth *The Art of War;* Lu Buwei was banished to Shu but his *Lü-lan* has been handed down through the ages; while Han Feizi was held prisoner in Qin, he wrote "The Difficulties of Disputation" and "The Sorrow of Standing Alone"; most of the three hundred poems of the *Book of Odes* were written when the sages and worthies poured forth their anger and dissatisfaction.[2]

Sima Qian cited these works of history and literature to show the role of suffering and persecution in the production of great writing. Historical writings such as these address humanity's fortunes and misfortunes, joys and sorrows, good and evil acts. They question the nature of human destiny as a whole, and they represent a search that strikes at the very heart of the human condition. This motif runs throughout Sima Qian's *Records of the Historian*.

When history is perceived as a probe into human destiny, the chronicle of past events can never stand independent of human beings, but must always involve them. History, in this view, is essentially the life story of the individual person.

There is a saying in Buddhism, "All the eighty-four thousand teachings are the daily record of the individual." "Eighty-four thousand" is a symbolic figure that indicates a very large number. The word "teachings" refers to the many doctrines that Shakyamuni Buddha preached in the course of his life. These countless doctrines in their totality must be accounted for in the vital force that is all parts of the life of the individual. Thus, like the Chinese view of history, this Buddhist approach requires people to stand on their own, unswayed by praise or blame, bravely facing whatever fate may await them.

The flow of history never ceases. In the words of Li Bai (also known as Li Po), one of China's greatest poets, "Heaven and earth are an inn for the ten thousand things of creation; time is the traveler of a hundred ages." The time has come for human beings to cease being content to play only a passive role in history. We need to recognize the importance of the free and independent individual in the making of history, and at the same time, link person to person in united movements that bind together the entire citizenry of the globe.

With the swift passing of time, the world is becoming a single entity in every sense of the word. China, Japan, or any country has a distinct history, but today all of us are passengers together on Spaceship Earth, faced with a common destiny. From now on, every person's history is that of the world as a whole. To meet the coming century with hope and confidence, no matter how unpredictable the flow of events may seem, we must once and for all learn to look upon history as the human drama in which people play the decisive role. At the same time, we must all recognize that, as fellow members of the global community, we need a sense of solidarity appropriate to the citizens of a single world.

Let me close by congratulating Fudan University on its eighty-year tradition of excellence in training men and women of talent. It is my sincere hope that, for the sake of China and the world at large, it will continue its educational research and activities with even greater vigor and success in the future.

NOTES

1. Friedrich Nietzsche, *Niiche Zenshu* (The Collected Works of Nietsche), trans. Yukiyoshi Ogura (Tokyo: Riso Sha Ltd., 1964), 2:99.
2. Sima Qian, *Shiki,* trans. Shigeki Kaizuka (Tokyo: Chuokoron-sha, 1968), 35.

PART III

~

Religion and
Our Time

~~~

A Godless Civilization

*A speech delivered at Peking University, Beijing,
April 22, 1980*

Vice-President Ji Xianlin, Vice-President Wang Zhuxi, and the faculty and student body of Peking University have made it possible for me to address you today. I am grateful for this opportunity to share with you some ideas I have formed about the way views of humankind are going to affect our world.

A few weeks ago, Dr. Kojiro Yoshikawa, a prominent Japanese authority on Chinese literature, passed away. I am sure there are many people in China who are acquainted with him and his work. In one of his books, he describes China as possessing a "godless civilization." Certainly no idea in the Chinese civilization or culture corresponds to the transcendent Judeo-Christian or Islamic concept of God. Furthermore, whereas other Asian countries, including Japan and India, have preserved a vast body of ancient myths, China seems to have been one of the first countries to divest itself of mythology. Confucius, the *Analects* tells us, "never talked of prodigies, feats of strength, disorders or spiritual beings"[1]; the same earthbound inclination seems to run through Chinese civilization as a whole. In the Confucian sense, the phrase "godless civilization" strikes me as extremely apt.

113

A Particular Approach to the Universal

What view does Chinese civilization take toward humans and the world in which they live? To generalize on the basis of my very inadequate knowledge of the subject, I would suggest that "viewing the universal in light of the particular" might characterize the Chinese approach.

As an example of what I mean, at the beginning of the biography section of *Shiji* (Records of the Historian), Sima Qian cites the popular belief that it is heaven's way to have no favorites, but to be always on the side of the good man. He goes on to show how history subverts this view by giving examples of good men who were destroyed, and evil men who flourished. His own reaction is contained in the famous words: "I find myself in much perplexity. Is this so-called Way of Heaven right or wrong?" It is a passage that is familiar to readers in Japan, too.

I do not intend to go into just what is meant by the term "Way of Heaven." No doubt, it reflects both Confucian and Taoist philosophy, but from the standpoint of our own era, it smacks of feudalistic ideology. At the same time, the very existence of such a concept testifies to the longing of ancient people for a definition of universal principles. And that desire to discover a universal law or principle underlying and linking people and the natural world is by no means peculiar to Chinese; it is common to human society everywhere.

In the passage I quoted, Sima Qian calls into question the validity of the "Way of Heaven" as a universal principle; it does not hold up in the light of particular historical events. The historian also spoke from personal experience. A close friend, Li Ling was a general who had been forced to surrender in battle, which infuriated the emperor. When Sima Qian stood up in defense of his friend in the presence of the emperor, he was condemned to be castrated. The Li Ling affair and its consequences inflicted a terrible blow. The bitterness and resentment that Sima Qian felt as a result of his punishment are reflected in numerous places in his writings. Above all, this extremely painful event forced him to make a personal evaluation of good and bad, right and wrong. At issue in his question concerning the Way of Heaven was not doubts about the principle as a whole, but whether or not his particular "Way of Heaven"—the tragedy that had befallen him as an individual—was right. It is in this sense that Sima Qian offers an example of the Chinese tendency to view the universal in light of the particular.

By contrast, societies in which the concept of God constitutes the philosophical cornerstone tend to view the particular in light of the universal. God directs the destiny of the world from a realm far removed from that of human beings, and we can observe how the absolute, universal deity realizes divine providence by finding it in the world in which we live. The God-human relationship is one-sided, in that the human role is strictly passive. In such a system, it is unthinkable to question the nature of the "Way of Heaven" in the manner that Sima Qian did. Such questioning became acceptable in Europe only in the latter years of the nineteenth century, when the "death of God" had been openly proclaimed.

Accordingly, when Europeans contemplated the human and natural worlds, they inevitably viewed them in an analytical way, looking at them through the refracting glass of the concept of God. The idea of God as a medium through which to view the world did not transplant well to cultures with different histories and traditions. Europeans resorted to coercion in attempting to force their God on others, and their efforts produced an aggressive and racist colonialism thinly disguised behind a veil of religious zeal.

An Ecumenical Heritage

Because of their tendency to view the universal in terms of the particular, Chinese have been able to do without any mediating concepts such as monotheism and have attempted to extract underlying principles of universal validity directly from reality itself. In his later years, the British historian Arnold J. Toynbee predicted that China would become a focal civilization in world history, bolstered by the ecumenical attitude developed by the Chinese people over thousands of years. Toynbee, who was critical of Christianity, saw in this venerable Chinese tradition a kind of budding cosmopolitanism that promises to overtake the very different and aggressive universalism of Europe.

I do not mean to gloss over the harsh realities of Chinese history. China, too, has experienced internal dissension, revolts, foreign aggression, repeated floods, droughts, and so on. All these have brought untold misery to the people. The revolutionary movements that have arisen in China in the present century, also painful in their own way, have been attempts not only to throw off colonial domination but also to rid the nation of the old feudal system, which, like a persistent disease, poisoned the hearts and minds of many generations of Chinese.

The spiritual legacy of the Chinese people has evolved over many centuries. But it is neither easy nor always advisable to attempt to modify the ingrained ethos of a people. That ethos, rather, should be carefully directed into constructive and beneficial channels, if China is to help build a bright future for itself, Asia, and the world.

When I look at portraits of the writer Lü Xun active in the first decades of this century, I sense the clarity of vision with which he saw into the basic character of the Chinese people. He sought to put aside any intervening medium in order to observe reality just as it is. When he depicted human beings, he stripped away every pretense and superficial decoration to capture a true likeness of the people. An enthusiastic reader of his works, I am especially moved by the conclusion of *A Madman's Diary,* which deals with the shameless ways in which people destroy each other. Lü Xun likens these acts of destruction to cannibalism. "Perhaps there are still children who have not eaten men? Save the children . . ." the protagonist of the story cries.[2] The moral thrust of the passage pierces the reader's heart.

Again, in his *True Story of Ah Q,* which depicts the lowest rung of peasants, he writes: "But our hero [Ah Q] was not so spineless. He was always exultant. This may be a proof of the moral supremacy of China over the rest of the world."[3] This simple passage is a striking portrayal of the true nature of the common people, who, though mired in ignorance and poverty, manage to make their way through life like tough weeds. The strength and innate honesty of Lü Xun's characters remind me of the young delinquent Parisian in *Les Misérables* by Victor Hugo. In this character, Hugo portrayed a kind of incorruptibility that was born of the ideas sweeping Paris in his time.

Lü Xun's literary movement cannot be said to have been entirely successful. Yet I am certain that the tasks that concerned him throughout his life are being faithfully carried out in the new China of today. The novelist Ba Jin, whom I had occasion to meet recently in Japan, has declared that he wrote "in order to combat my enemies." He went on to say at that time, "What are my enemies? Every kind of old, traditional concept, every irrational system that impedes social progress and the expansion of the human spirit, everything that destroys love." Ba Jin was indeed a fighter, like Lü Xun, in the battle against anyone or anything that might harm the people.

A New Type of People

"Serve the People!" and "Be a Servant of the People!" are among the slogans that have appeared so often in China since the 1949 revolution. To me, they promise the emergence of a new kind of people who will create a fresh page in history.

Another slogan, *shishi qiushi,* "to seek the truth in reality," is reminiscent of the Chinese tendency to view the universal in light of the particular. Its underlying logic appears to follow the same pattern as Sima Qian's query on the nature of the Way of Heaven. Both relate intimately to one of the finest elements in the spiritual legacy of China: the conviction that one must confront reality directly and, on that basis, decide how reality can best be reconstituted.

We are living in a period of profound change and upheaval. The late premier Zhou Enlai remarked that the last quarter of the present century is likely to be a period of crucial importance. In times like these, people across the world must form bonds that transcend national boundaries if they are not to be visited once again by the horrors of war. As Joseph Needham says in the introduction to his monumental *Science and Civilization in China:*

> We are living in the dawn of a new universalism, which, if humanity survives the dangers attendant on control by irresponsible men of sources of power hitherto unimaginable, will

unite the working peoples of all races in a community both catholic and cooperative. [4]

We must have a new type of people, a new image of people, to play the leading role in the development of this universalism. I firmly believe that China, with its long history and focus on reality, possesses the boundless energy that is needed to help inaugurate the new era.

NOTES

1. *The Analects of Confucius,* trans. Arthur Waley (New York: Random House, Inc., 1989), 127.

2. *Selected Stories of Lü Hsun,* trans. Yang Hsien-yi & Gladys Yang (San Francisco: China Books & Periodicals, Inc., 1994), 18.

3. Ibid., 79.

4. Joseph Needham, *Science and Civilization in China* (Cambridge: The University Press, 1954), 9.

The Enduring Self

*A speech delivered at the University of California
at Los Angeles, April 1, 1974*

It is a great pleasure to have this opportunity to speak at the University of California at Los Angeles, an institution that carries on the finest traditions of higher learning. For this privilege, I thank President Charles E. Young, Vice-president Norman Miller, the faculty and students, men and women who will guide your country into the next country.

The Path of Moderation

Arnold J. Toynbee, historian and philosopher, remains deeply concerned about the fate of humanity in the coming century. Over the past few years, I have had the opportunity to engage in an extended series of dialogues with this great thinker. Our discussions have been a source of personal enrichment and intense intellectual stimulation for me.*

Toynbee sets a demanding example of industry for the members of the younger generation. At the age of eighty-five, he rises at six o'clock every morning, and by nine o'clock he is at the desk in his study, ready for work. I once saw him seated at that desk, and was struck by the beauty of his old age. Toynbee related to me an episode about the industrious third-century Roman emperor Lucius Septimus Severus, who, on the day of his death, though seriously ill and still commanding his troops in the cold of northern England, gave his men the word *laboramus,* or "let us work," as their motto. The British historian adopted this as his own, he told me. That, I thought, was the secret of his enduring vigor and his determination to continue his tasks. Toynbee has the kind of beauty that stems from his lifelong intellectual struggle and soul-searching.

Our talks ranged over an immense field of topics, including civilization, life, learning, education, literature, art, science, international affairs, modern society, human nature, and women. Toynbee was urgently concerned with the course of events after his own death. He very much wanted to leave behind an inspiring message for those who will follow. His desire to assist future generations was the dominant theme of our discussions. I hope that, at its close, my life will reveal no less intense a dedication to the well-being of posterity.

According to Toynbee, the twentieth century's intoxication with technology has led to the poisoning of our environment and has created the possibility that humanity may destroy itself. He believes that any solution to the current crisis depends on self-control. Mastery of the self, however, cannot be achieved through either extreme self-indulgence or extreme asceticism. The people of the twenty-first century must learn to walk the middle path, the way of moderation.

I find this injunction to be especially congenial, because the ideals of moderation and the middle way are pervasive elements in Mahayana Buddhism. Moderation, in this sense, refers to a way of life that is a synthesis of materialism and spirituality. The path of moderation is the only answer to the current crisis of civilization.

To follow that path, however, humankind requires a reliable guide. Toynbee and I pondered some methodological problems as well, but we agreed that preoccupation with techniques will get us nowhere. In searching for the kind of guide needed today, we must return to such basic issues as the nature of humanity and the meaning of existence, both of which necessarily lead to the question of the essential quality of life. Knowing what we really are, what life is, is fundamental to the understanding of cultures and civilizations. When the people of the twenty-first century are able to perceive the true nature of life, humanity will move away from infatuation with technology and create a civilization that is humane in the richest, fullest meaning of the word.

One of the primary teachings of Buddhism is that human life is a composite of sorrows; the burden of birth, the agony of growing old, the pain of illness, the grief of the death of loved ones, and ultimately one's own death. These are the most basic sufferings, but there are others. Pleasant times are fleeting; we must all face the sadness of seeing them end. In today's society there are many causes for unhappiness; the presence of racial and ethnic discrimination, for example, and the widening gap between rich and poor.

In our lives, grief and pain occur for many different reasons, but what is the cause for sorrow itself? The Buddhist answer is that nothing in the universe is constant, and that sorrow is the result of the human inability to understand that basic principle. The transient nature of all phenomena is self-evident. The young must grow old, the healthy become ill, all living creatures must eventually die, and all that has form ultimately decays. As Heraclitus said almost two and a half millennia ago, all things are in a constant state of flux; nothing in the universe remains the same, but everything shifts from instant to instant like the current of a mighty river. In spite of what our senses may suggest, nothing is immutable. Moreover, it is a basic tenet of Buddhism that clinging fast to the illusion of permanence causes the sufferings of the human spirit.

Attachment to the Transient

To hope for permanence is only human. We all want beauty and youth to last forever. As we work to acquire the good things of the world, we trust that whatever wealth we may accumulate will endure. Still, we realize that, no matter how hard we work and no matter how large our bank accounts grow, we cannot, as the saying goes, take it with us. Recognizing this, we continue to work in order to enjoy the benefits of our earnings, and naturally we want to enjoy them for as long as we can. This is one source of sorrow; we cannot keep the fruits of our labor forever. The same is true of our human relationships. No matter how great the love one feels or how much one wants it to endure, a day of parting must come. The loss of a loved one—husband, wife, parent, child, friend—causes the greatest spiritual suffering that we are called upon to face.

Attachment to people leads to grief; attachment to things and the greedy desire for material goods can be the source of conflict; attachment to power often leads to war. Too much attachment to one's own life can cause a descent into a morass of worry and fear. Most of us actually do not worry constantly about the imminence of death. On the contrary, we carry out the affairs of our daily lives more or less convinced that we will live on for the indefinite future. There are people, however, who are unable to assume this blindly optimistic attitude. Possessed by a frantic desire to stay alive as long as they can, they are consumed by the fear of death, aging, and illness.

No matter what we do, human life keeps changing. Our own bodies, which represent a physical manifestation of the incessant transformation of the universe, must someday die. To live our lives sanely and with meaning, we must face our fate coolly and without fear. In Buddhist terms, the path to enlightenment cannot be traveled without the acceptance of constant, universal change.

But it would be wrong to dismiss entirely the usefulness of attachments to things, even though they are impermanent. As long as we are alive and human, it is perfectly natural that we strive to preserve life, value the love of others, and enjoy the material benefits of this earth. In certain times and places, Buddhist teachings have been understood as directed toward the severance of all connection with the passions and desires of the world. They have also been seen as opposed to, or at least hindering, the advancement of civilization.

Buddhism, in fact, has penetrated deeply into the Japanese culture and psyche. It may be that the lack of advanced technology in some of the Buddhist nations can be attributed in part to the doctrine of transience; this, however, is only one aspect of the philosophy. Essential Buddhist teachings do not urge severance from this-worldly desires or isolation from all attachments. They preach neither resignation nor nihilism. Buddhist thought at its core is a teaching of the immutable Law, the essential life, the unchanging essence that underlies all the transience of actuality, that which unifies and gives rhythm to all things and generates the desires and attachments of human life.

Each of us consists of a lesser self and a greater self. To be blinded by temporary circumstance and tortured by inordinate desires is to exist only for the lesser self. To live for the larger self means to recognize the universal principle behind all things and, thus enlightened, rise above the transience of the phenomena of the world. What is this larger self? It is the basic principle of the whole universe. At the same time, it is the Law that generates the many manifestations of and activities in human life. Arnold Toynbee, describing the greater self as the ultimate spiritual reality of the universe, considers the Buddhist concept of the Law to be closer to the truth than notions of anthropomorphic gods.

To live for the greater self does not mean abandoning the lesser self, for the lesser self is able to act only because of the existence of the greater self. The effect of that relationship is to motivate the desires and attachments common to all human beings to stimulate the advancement of civilization. If wealth were not attractive, economic growth would not take place. If humans had not struggled to overcome the natural elements, science could not have flourished. Without the mutual attachment and conflicts characteristic of relationships between the sexes, literature would have been deprived of one of its most lyrical and enduring themes.

Although some branches of Buddhism have taught that people must try to free themselves from desire, sometimes even condoning self-immolation as a way of escaping this life, such an approach is not representative of the highest elements of Buddhist thought. Desire and sorrow are essential aspects of life; they cannot be eliminated. Desire and all it implies constitutes a generative, driving force. Nevertheless, desire (and the lesser self which it affects) must be correctly oriented. In striving to discover the greater self, the genuine Buddhist approach is not to suppress or wipe out the lesser self, but to control and direct it so as to help lift civilization to better, higher levels.

Beyond Life and Death

Buddhism teaches that all things will pass and that death must be faced with open eyes. Even so, the Buddha was not a prophet of resignation, but a man who had attained full understanding of the Law of impermanence. He taught the need to face death and change without fear, because he knew that the immutable Law is the source of life and of value. None of us can escape death, but Buddhism leads us to see that behind death is the eternal, unchanging, greater life that is the Law. Secure in the absolute faith that this is the truth, we can face both our own demise and the impermanence of all worldly things with courage.

According to the Buddhist Law, since life itself is eternal and universal, life and death are merely two aspects of the same thing. Neither is in any way subordinate to the other. There is a Japanese term, *ku,* that helps us to understand the ultimate, eternal life governing individual living and dying. *Ku* transcends the concept of space and time, for it signifies limitless potential; it is the essence from which all things are made manifest and to which all things return. Being everlasting and all-pervasive, it surpasses the space-time framework. In our many discussions of eternity, Toynbee said that he felt in the idea of *ku* an approximation of what he calls the ultimate spiritual reality.

It is impossible to do justice to the nature of *ku* in so short a time, but I should like to make a few points. First of all, *ku* is not nonexistence. In fact, it is neither existence nor nonexistence. These two terms represent human interpretations of reality based on the space-time axes by which we ordinarily gauge our experiences and environments. *Ku* is more profound, more essential; it is a fundamental reality. Its nature may be illustrated by reference to the universal experiences of human development. The psychological and physical changes which take place as the individual grows from infancy to maturity are so great that the entire person seems to be transformed. Yet throughout this process, there is a self that unites mind and body, and remains relatively constant. We are not always aware of this self, which is manifested on both the physical and the mental planes, but it is the fundamental reality that lies beyond the realm of existence and nonexistence.

According to Buddhist philosophy, this enduring self is directly connected with the great web of cosmic life, and so it is capable of operating eternally—now in the life phase and now in the death phase. This is why Buddhism interprets life and death as one. Since the lesser self is included in the greater self, each of us partakes of immutable cosmic life while living in the world of transience and change.

Breaking the Bonds of Desire

Unfortunately, modern societies seem to be swayed almost completely by the desires of the lesser self. Human greed has produced an immense, sophisticated technological system that has had devastating costs in environmental pollution and depletion of the natural resources of the planet. Attachment to things and desires and passions have led to the creation of huge buildings, sprawling transportation networks, and ominously potent weaponry. If the attitudes that have produced these things proceed unchecked, the self-destruction of humankind seems inevitable. Nevertheless, I remain hopeful that the current worldwide tendency to reflect on what is happening in society and to reclaim humane values are signs that we are at last searching for our own nature as human beings.

No matter how superb one's intellectual abilities, a person is no more than an animal if he or she is dominated entirely by passions and the pursuit of the impermanent. It is now time for all individuals to look toward the enduring aspects of life and so live in a way that will bring forth true human value. How can this be done, now and in the future? Once again, Arnold Toynbee suggests a way. He referred to the greed and desires of the lesser self as diabolic desire; the will to become one with the greater self is loving desire. He insisted that people can control the former and give free rein to the latter only if they exercise constant vigilance and self-restraint.

In the next century, I hope that human civilization will break away from its bondage to the lesser self and move forward with an understanding of the permanent self that abides behind the fleeting existence of the material world. This is the only way for us to be worthy of our humanity and for civilization to become truly humane. The coming century should be devoted to respect for life in the widest sense, for the Law behind the universe is life itself.

The basis on which people choose to operate will determine the success or failure of civilization in the future. Will we elect to flounder in the mire of selfish desires and greed? Or will we walk safely on the firm ground of enlightenment, fully aware of the greater self? The realization of the dreams for the well-being and happiness of all depends entirely on our willingness to concentrate on the immutable, unchanging, powerful reality that is the Law and the greater life. We have arrived at the point where this decision must be made.

Our time is a transition from one century to the next, but it is also much more. It is a time when all of us must decide whether to become human in the richest, fullest sense of the word. At the risk of sounding extreme, it seems to me that in the past, people have rarely advanced much beyond the stage of an intelligent animal. Seven hundred years ago, Nichiren Daishonin, the founder of the religious group of which I am a member, wrote of the "talented beast." Considering the actions of human beings in the modern world, these words are particularly meaningful. It is my belief that we must become more than an intelligent or talented animal. It is time for us to become active in the spiritual sense as we struggle to attain an understanding of the greater self and of cosmic life.

Each individual person must find his or her own way. I have found mine in Buddhism, and with faith in its teachings, long ago I embarked upon the journey of life. Young people, now standing at an important turning point in history, are capable of building much for the good of humankind. In offering fragments of the wisdom of Buddhism, I will be very happy if what I have said is of assistance to them as they choose their paths to the future.

NOTES

1. Arnold J. Toynbee (1889-1975) was still living when Mr. Ikeda spoke at UCLA.—Eds.

Gandhism and the Modern World

*A speech delivered at the National Museum of India, New Delhi,
February 11, 1992*

I am grateful to Gandhi Smriti and Darshan Samiti for inviting me
to speak at the National Museum. It is an honor to be their guest,
for through their labors the immortal spirit of Mahatma Gandhi is
being transmitted from the time and place where he lived into the
future and out to the entire world.

The Foresight of Gandhi

No one will deny that our world needs the spirit of Mahatma
Gandhi. We are in a period of momentous change, a major transition on a scale that occurs perhaps once in a century. In the
Soviet Union, Mikhail Gorbachev unleashed historical forces in
the process of implementing perestroika, and, like waters bursting
a dike, those forces inundated the system that had set them in
motion. While upheaval has characterized the final years of other
centuries, the changes we have witnessed these past few years—
from the collapse of the Berlin Wall to the dissolution of the
Soviet Union—have far outstripped the expectations of any historian.

On the one hand, these events have given power to the idea that no form of authority is capable of smothering indefinitely the voices of ordinary people who are struggling to attain freedom. On the other, so many transitions at once threaten to set us adrift in new and uncharted currents of history, bereft of any guiding ideology or principle. Without guidance, chaos looms, making it all the more urgent that we listen to the voice of Mahatma Gandhi quietly addressing us, as if from the still depths that lie beneath the churning, turbulent surface of history-in-the-making.

In December of 1931, Gandhi wrote to the French writer Romain Rolland who was convalescing at Lac Leman in Switzerland:

> What is happening in Russia is an enigma. I have not discussed Russia very much, but I have a deep mistrust of the ultimate success of the experiment being carried out there. It seems to me that it is a challenge to nonviolence. It appears to be succeeding, but behind its success lies force, violence. . . . When Indians are exposed to Russian influence, they are led into extreme intolerance.[1]

To many of the people who saw fascism as a growing, ominous threat at that time, the communist experiment in the Soviet Union appeared as a beacon of hope for humanity. In 1931, the propensity to violence and terror that made up the dark side of Bolshevism had not yet been fully exposed to the world. It was not strange in those years that such an ardent pacifist as Rolland should see it as his mission to link the revolutions of Gandhi and Lenin, "So that the two may come together at this hour to overthrow the old world and found a new order."[2]

Given the historical circumstances and the limited information available to him, it is indeed remarkable that Gandhi was able to perceive the intolerance that has since proved to be one of the most notable afflictions of Bolshevism. His prescience came from a unique clarity of vision that was deepened and refined through the accumulated experience of his lifetime. In August of 1991, the vast media networks let people all over the world witness the enormous statue of Feliks Dzerzhinski, founder of the KGB, being pulled down and trampled by the citizens of Moscow. As I watched that extraordinary image, I was once more struck by the sureness of Gandhi's vision which, unclouded by prejudice, enabled him to discern the essential nature of people and events.

As we approach the end of a century which has seen unprecedented war and violence, our common goal must be the creation of a world at peace. At this critical juncture, this great philosopher and apostle of nonviolence, whose spiritual legacy is one of humanity's priceless treasures, should be our guide. I would like to offer some personal reflections on Mahatma Gandhi, focusing on his optimism, activism, populism, and the holistic nature of his vision.

Optimism

One of Gandhi's extraordinary gifts was his relentless and unshakable hope for the future. Since ancient times, the mark of virtually every great figure or widely respected personality, whether philosopher or statesman, has been an unshakable belief in the essential goodness of the universe. It would be very difficult, however, to find anyone comparable to Gandhi. His every action and accomplishment bore witness to his total concern for others and the presence of a pure and refreshing optimism, untainted by the slightest hint of showmanship. As he himself said:

> I remain an optimist, not that there is any evidence that I can give that right is going to prosper, but because of my unflinching faith that right must prosper in the end.[3]

On another occasion, he stated, "My optimism rests on my belief in the infinite possibilities of the individual to develop nonviolence."[4] As these passages suggest, Gandhi's faith was absolute, not relative. It was never contingent on an analysis of objective conditions or a prognosis of future events. His belief in nonviolence and justice grew out of his absolute trust in humanity. His was an unconditional faith, developed through a rigorous process of introspection in which he probed the very depths of his being. The indestructible conviction he achieved was something that not even death could take from him. His method represents the essence of the type of deductive reasoning that, in the characteristic way of Asian philosophy, always begins in a reflective return to the self. Because it was unconditional, his optimism knew no deadlock or impasse, but promised a vision of unbounded hope and success. He taught that there can be no defeat in nonviolence, and that violence can never lead to victory. In his quiet words, we sense an indomitable self-confidence, the triumph of a soul that has achieved true self-mastery.

Gandhi's state of mind, forged in the crucible of so many trials, was pure, like the pellucid cobalt sky spreading free above dark and heavy clouds. I believe he maintained such equanimity throughout his life—even as he fasted in prison; even as he faced the difficult question of how to confront the fascist threat; even as he sought a resolution to the violent communal clashes in Bengal and Calcutta. It was this spirit that sustained his optimism as he attempted to teach the Indian people the ultimate human virtue of nonviolence.

Gandhi's pacifism was not the cowardly or servile nonviolence of the weak, for it was founded on the quiet strength that comes from courage. We find the true essence of Gandhi's legacy in his spiritual strength and conviction in the pursuit of his ideals. He personified a clear principle that cannot be modified and retain its integrity. Deviation from it, even if the results were immediate success, would lead to an adulteration of Gandhism and the substitution of something no longer worthy of the name. Repudiation of violence was the essential characteristic of this individual who was, in Rolland's words "religious by nature . . . a political leader by necessity."[5] To Gandhi, pacifism constituted proof of our humanity; the question of worldly success or failure was always of secondary importance.

At times, Gandhi's intensely philosophical way of life was a source of perplexity for comrades and sympathizers, such as Nehru and Rolland, who were unable to attain such heights. Indeed, considered in the short term, Gandhi's advocacy of passive resistance to the Nazis might seem idealistic to the point of being unrealistic. The history of the postwar period has shown us, however, that in the long run, his way is the best. We must acknowledge the truth spoken by this voice in the wilderness—a truth he continued to assert even during war—that nonviolence offers the only means by which true liberty and democracy can be realized. Given the mistrust and pessimism of our age, Gandhi's brand of optimism, his proudly declared faith in humanity, is still desperately needed.

Gradualist Activism

A second aspect of Gandhi's legacy is his activism. Throughout his life, Gandhi was a man of unusual action. The range and scope of his efforts were incomparably wider than those of other advocates of nonviolence, such as Tolstoy. Once, when a Brahman suggested that he enter a life of meditation, Gandhi is said to have replied that while his days were devoted to efforts to attain the spiritual liberation of enlightenment, he felt no need to withdraw to a cave for that purpose. The cave, he said, was something which he carried about with him. The quintessential Gandhian humor of this response provides a wonderful glimpse into the character of the barefoot saint.

Gandhi's activism should not be confused with mere action, something that animals perform equally well, if not better. Rather, his industry and energy more properly resemble spiritual practice. Gandhi was inspired by the inner urging of his conscience. He did what was necessary and then examined his accomplishments with love and modesty in order to judge where they might have fallen short or gone too far. Although he had courage and resolution, he also had the humility to recognize reality. He was, therefore, entirely free from the arrogance that seeks a monopoly on legitimacy. His convictions were unshakable, but he never sought to ground his beliefs merely in theoretical or logical consistency. Their base was in the depths of his own soul; this was the foundation for the generosity of spirit and tolerance that enabled him to embrace all people. Good, he said, travels at a snail's pace. On another occasion he wrote: "Nonviolence is a plant of slow growth. It grows imperceptibly, but surely."[6] The weight of those words and the profound impression they make derive from being the quiet expression of an individual credo held by a man whose beliefs and actions were in complete accord.

Our image of Gandhi the activist stands in stark contrast with our impression of the social and political revolutionaries who followed twentieth-century radical ideologies. Bolshevism, for example, has nurtured many intense revolutionaries who, while dedicated and idealistic, have too often been limited by a narrow-minded dogmatism. All too frequently, such people have not hesitated to resort to violence when they felt it was necessary to accomplish their goals. In his most famous work, *Doctor Zhivago,* Boris Pasternak denounces the apostles of radical ideology, saying that they "have never understood a thing about life . . . have never felt its breath, its heartbeat."[7]

Saumyendranath Tagore, nephew of the poet Rabindranath Tagore, was apparently a tragic example of this malady. Although originally an adherent of Gandhism, he later became a communist who worked against Gandhi and virulently criticized him. In his diaries, Romain Rolland describes the young Tagore who visited him:

> He is without doubt a generous young idealist, very sincere and ready to sacrifice everything for his faith. Which makes it all the more sad to see these fine forces, intelligent and pure, hurling themselves against the greatest and purest of Indians. The fatal madness afflicting the souls of individuals swept up in the whirlwind of revolutions![8]

There are some who, having observed the chain of events leading up to the dissolution of the Soviet Union, regard the Russian people as having brought to its ultimate conclusion a process set in motion by the French Revolution. In a certain sense, the fall of Soviet communism can be seen as the passing of the ideology of radical rationalism that began with the French Revolution and was carried on by the Russian Revolution. Early on, Gandhi saw the underlying weakness of the rationalist ideology: "Rationalists," he wrote, "are admirable beings; rationalism is a hideous monster when it claims for itself omnipotence."[9] Against this background, the enduring nobility of Gandhi's life, with its adherence to a philosophy of gradualist activism, is all the more striking.

Paternal Populism

A third element of Gandhi's legacy is his populism, his extraordinary communion with the mass of "ordinary people." In our increasingly democratic world, there are many leaders who invoke the name of "the people." How many of them, however, can honestly be described as working on the side of and for the sake of the people? Too often it seems that they are in fact merely "playing the crowd," which they secretly scorn and seek to use for their own purposes. In contrast, Gandhi was a genuine friend and father-figure to the common folk. He had a profound grasp of the popular mind and lived a selfless and devoted life among ordinary Indians, whose joys and sorrows he made his own. All these qualities earned him the title Mahatma (great soul). The following passage clearly demonstrates his limitless love and willingness to suffer with the people.

> Why should he [God] have chosen me, an imperfect instrument, for such a mighty experiment? I think he deliberately did so. He had to serve the poor, dumb, ignorant millions. A perfect man might have been their despair. When they found that one with their failings was marching on towards *ahimsa* (nonviolence), they too had confidence in their own capacity.[10]

Nichiren Daishonin, founder of the Buddhist faith that inspires Soka Gakkai International, was born the son of a poor fisherman. But he took pride in his origins when he raised the banner of a Buddhist teaching dedicated to the masses. Gandhi's attitude toward his fellow human beings strikes me as being profoundly similar to the Bodhisattva Way revealed in Mahayana Buddhism.

And yet, Gandhi's relationship with the people was not limited to the "maternal" aspects of affection, love, and compassion for the suffering of the oppressed. He demonstrated a stern paternal love in his recognition of the need for training and discipline. He knew that only by developing the discipline of self-control could people truly understand nonviolence and use it to overcome their weakness and realize their own strength. That conviction must have sustained him in his unconditional commitment to the advancement of the huge numbers of Indians who made up the lower classes in his day.

"I have all along believed," he wrote, "that what is possible for one is possible for all . . . . My experiments have not been conducted in the closet, but in the open."[11] The phrase "possible for one" refers to the nonviolence of the strong and courageous, the practice of which "implies as complete self-purification as is humanly possible."[12] He struggled always to make the lofty ideal of nonviolence attainable by everyone. All his life, he ceaselessly urged and encouraged people to be strong, while he organized them into a mass movement on a scale without precedent or parallel. Einstein praised him as the greatest political genius of our age; I personally would substitute the words "human history" for "our age." His remarkable gifts shone in the brilliant success of the Salt March, which was carried out despite skepticism and doubts among many of his associates. Underlying and animating his political genius was a unique and penetrating understanding of the people.

One of those closest to Gandhi and able to directly observe his qualities was his friend and ally, Jawaharlal Nehru. In *The Discovery of India,* Nehru describes Gandhi's advent as "a powerful current of fresh air, like a beam of light." Gandhi brought a dramatic transformation in the public consciousness. In Nehru's words, Gandhi "pierced the darkness and removed the scales from our eyes, like a whirl-wind that upset many things but most of all the working of people's minds."[13]

If the people were to be strengthened and invigorated, they must first be liberated from the fear of authority created by long years of colonial rule. This fear was often accompanied by the weakness of cowardice and resignation. Gandhi offered them advice, telling them that goodness and strength must be coupled with wisdom and intelligence to be effective:

Goodness must be joined with knowledge. Mere goodness is not of much use. . . . One must cultivate the fine discriminating quality which goes with spiritual courage and character.[14]

Nehru called Gandhi's simple injunction "Be not afraid!" his greatest gift to the Indian people. It is the action of ordinary citizens in freeing themselves from the fear of power and authority that heralds the dawn of a truly democratic era. Gandhi's message will continue to illuminate future centuries as a gift not only to the people of India, but to all humanity.

A Holistic Vision

Finally, I want to touch on the holistic nature of Gandhi's thought and its larger implications for civilization. If we were to pinpoint the central flaw of modern Western civilization, it would probably have to be the sense of isolation and fragmentation that pervades all areas of life and society. The Western worldview draws lines of distinction between human beings and the universe, between humankind and nature, between the individual and society, between different peoples, good and evil, means and end, sacred and secular, and so forth. As a result of this ever greater fragmentation, the individual human being has been pushed into a state of isolation. Modern history has witnessed the acceleration of the pursuit of equality, freedom, and dignity, and at the same time, increasing personal alienation.

The ideas that Gandhi advocated with his whole being and throughout his life are the antithesis to our modern isolation. Although his critique of civilization (symbolized by his famous *charka,* or spinning wheel) may seem extreme, his global—even cosmic—sensibility suffusing his every word and action is an invaluable legacy. His was a holistic approach to life that, turning away from fragmentation and isolation, aspired to integration and harmony.

> I could not be leading a religious life unless I identified myself with the whole of mankind, and that I could not do unless I took part in politics. The whole gamut of man's activities today constitutes an indivisible whole. You cannot divide social, economic, political and purely religious work into watertight compartments. I do not know any religion apart from human

activity. It provides a moral basis to all other activities which they would otherwise lack, reducing life to a maze of sound and fury signifying nothing.[15]

His point here is perfectly clear and is also consistent with the philosophy of Mahayana Buddhism, which stresses that daily life and religion are an indivisible whole. While separation of church and state is an immutable principle of modern government, it does not mean that religion must restrict itself to the private, inner life of the individual. Rather, religion is a source of energy and inspiration for human activities of all descriptions. Gandhi called for a world where essential religious values would enrich and enhance all aspects of human society.

In 1979, I visited India and met Jaya Prakash Narayan, one of Gandhi's closest disciples. We talked at his country residence in Patna on the middle reaches of the Ganges River. Narayan had previously advanced the concept of "total revolution" and, as we talked, we agreed that the first step had to be a "human revolution" involving the inner spiritual transformation of each individual. This, in turn, would generate reformation in politics, education, and culture. Although he was battling illness at the time, there was a strength and firmness in his voice that belied the seriousness of his condition. At the time, I felt that Narayan represented the unbroken heritage of Gandhi's living, breathing spirit which, strengthened by tribulation, was being passed on to the next generation.

More than thirty years ago, the American sociologist Daniel Bell predicted the coming of our present "post-ideological" age. In *The Winding Passage,* Bell wrote, "Will there be a return of the sacred, the rise of new religious modes? Of that I have no doubt."[16] This echoes the spirituality for which Gandhi appealed when he wrote, "Religion does not mean sectarianism. It means a belief in ordered moral government of the Universe."[17] Gandhi believed in the immense spiritual and religious potential that resides equally within each of us. He believed that we must not allow this inner source of energy and strength to lie dormant. We must, he insisted, rouse and awaken it.

Recognizing "no other God than Truth" and resolute in his rejection of sectarianism, Gandhi possessed just this kind of spiritual strength. It is the same spirituality that will heal and revive human hearts and minds deeply wounded by violent ideologies and open the way for a new chapter in human history.

When Dr. Radhakrishnan, director of the National Museum, visited Japan last autumn, our conversation at one point turned to the memories of our respective mentors and to the spiritual inheritance that is passed from teacher to disciple. My personal mentor was Josei Toda, second president of the Soka Gakkai. Born in 1900, Toda was thirty years younger than Mahatma Gandhi. During the second world war, when Gandhi was engaged in his final struggles in prison, Toda was also imprisoned for his opposition to the Japanese military authorities. Like Gandhi, Toda was a pacifist of profound conviction. It was he who taught me the exalted way of peace when I was nineteen, just after the war. President Toda was also a leader of the people, inspired by a deep sense of compassion. Finally, like Gandhi, he was a creative social reformer. All of the Soka Gakkai International's activities for peace, culture, and education stem from Toda's efforts and from the spirit he bequeathed us.

For forty-five years, I have devoted myself to Toda's legacy. It is my desire and determination to continue to develop a global network of spiritual solidarity directed toward a world without war. In this endeavor, I trust that I will have the company of my esteemed Indian friends. I know that, in these efforts, the image of Gandhi will always be in my heart.

In closing, I would like to share some lines by Rabindranath Tagore, who gave Gandhi the title of Mahatma. This poem is a paean to the eternal rhythm of life that animates all peoples, every society, and the universe itself.

The same stream of life that runs through my veins night and day runs through the world and dances in rhythmic measures. It is the same life that shoots in joy through the dust of the earth in numberless blades of grass and breaks into tumultuous waves of leaves and flowers.

It is the same life that is rocked in the ocean—cradle of birth and of death, in ebb and in flow.

I feel my limbs are made glorious by the touch of this world of life. And my pride is from the life-throb of ages dancing in my blood this moment.[18]

NOTES

1. Romain Rolland, *Romain Rolland and Gandhi Correspondence* (New Delhi: Publications Division, Ministry of Information and Broadcasting, Government of India, 1976), 180.

2. Ibid., 280.

3. Mahatma Gandhi, *All Men Are Brothers: Autobiographical Reflections* (New York: The Continuum Publishing Company, 1990), 70-71.

4. Mohandas Gandhi, *Gandhi on Non-Violence: Selected Texts from Non-Violence in Peace and War* (New York: New Directions Publishing Corp., 1965), 26.

5. Romain Rolland, *Mahatma Gandhi, The Man Who Became One with the Universal Being* (New York: The Century Co., 1924), 32.

6. Mahatma Gandhi, *The Collected Works of Mahatma Gandhi* (The Publications Division, Ministry of Information and Broadcasting, Government of India, 1958–73), 206.

7. Boris Pasternak, *Doctor Zhivago* (New York: Signet Books, 1960), 282.

8. Romain Rolland, *Romain Rolland and Gandhi Correspondence*, 295.

9. Mahatma Gandhi, *All Men Are Brothers*, 156.

10. Ibid., 46.

11. Ibid., 4.

12. Mohandas Gandhi, *Gandhi on Non-Violence*, 24.

13. Jawaharlal Nehru, *The Discovery of India* (New York: The John Day Co., 1946), 361.

14. Mohandas Gandhi, *Gandhi on Non-Violence*, 34.

15. Mahatma Gandhi, *All Men Are Brothers*, 63.

16. Daniel Bell, *The Winding Passage* (Cambridge: ABT Books, 1980), 347.

17. Mahatma Gandhi, *Harijan* (Bombay), 10 February 1940, 445.

18. Rabindranath Tagore, "Gitanjali" (LXIX) from *Collected Poems and Plays of Rabindranath Tagore* (New York: MacMillan, 1973), 33.

An Ethos of Symbiosis

A speech delivered at the Chinese Academy of Social Sciences,
Beijing, October 14, 1992

I am privileged to have this opportunity to speak before members of the respected and prestigious Chinese Academy of Social Sciences. I also deeply appreciate being named an honorary research professor of this academy. My gratitude goes to President Hu Sheng, members of the Academy, and all the distinguished guests gathered here today.

As President Hu reminded us, conditions around the world are becoming increasingly chaotic as we approach the twenty-first century. The late Chinese premier, Zhou Enlai, predicted that the world would soon see great changes, and we have seen his words come true. Since the collapse of the Cold War order, which was held in place by the rivalry between the United States and the Soviet Union, the global situation has been shifting so quickly that we dare not glance away for even a second. One development, however, has been steady and growing, and that is the new interest in East Asia—China, Japan, North and South Korea, Taiwan, and Hong Kong.

The principal reason for this increasing attention is the impressive economic record of the region. First Japan, and more recently, the so-called NIEs (newly industrialized economies) have been showing remarkable economic growth. That achievement, and the enormous vitality of China, make it clear that whatever uncertainties remain, East Asia will be a major center of the world economy in the twenty-first century.

But the new focus on East Asia spotlights much more than the economic realm. There is enormous interest in those aspects of culture that have contributed to or might explain the success story of East Asia. Cultural elements common to a given region form a "culture sphere." In Japan these days, one often finds such terms as "Confucian culture sphere" and "Chinese-ideograph culture sphere" being used in discussion or in print. Analysts in industrialized Western nations seem especially eager to study those cultural elements. In sum, I think it safe to say that the emphasis in approaches to East Asia is shifting away from the "hardware" to the "software" of development.

"We" Over "I"

How can one best characterize East Asian culture and spirituality, those elusive elements that are the heartbeat of its civilization? There is of course no simple answer, but if I were to propose a way of looking at the world that is shared throughout the region, I would single out an "ethos of symbiosis." I am talking about the kind of mentality that favors harmony over opposition, unity over division, "we" over "I." Practically, it is expressed as the idea that human beings should live in harmony with each other and with nature. By mutually supporting one another, the entire community flourishes. These beliefs are played out against the backdrop of a relatively temperate climate and beautiful natural surroundings.

There can be no argument that Confucianism is a major source of the "ethos of symbiosis." But we must distinguish between traditional Confucian tenets, such as the "three relations" and the "five practices,"[1] and the broader Confucian emphasis on the group over the individual. The former, more specific, teachings are meant to regulate relationships and behavior and tend to sanction the status quo of social hierarchies, rendering society rigid and stagnant. It was only natural that the May Fourth Movement vehemently attacked such a feudalistic ideology. These negative effects of Confucianism can be traced to its adoption as the official ideology, which almost made it a national religion, during the Han dynasty at the urging of Dong Zhongshu. As the history of Roman Catholicism also shows, when religion aligns itself with secular authorities and becomes the tool of the ruling class, it is cut off from the lives of the people and loses its roots, the source of its freshness and vitality.

What can a relic such as this, enveloped in the still air of an age long gone by, contribute to the civilization of the twenty-first century? This negative aspect of Confucianism is one reason that I have reservations about Japan's astonishing and loudly-trumpeted economic growth of the past few decades. Japan's achievement, supported by a philosophy based on teachings from another era, has involved great personal sacrifices and the minimization of individual human rights. This is a criticism frequently directed at Japan by Western observers, and there is solid ground for it. The doctrine of the absolute supremacy of the company is supported by a feudalistic, exclusivistic way of thinking that superficially resembles an ethos of symbiosis, but it is really something quite different: a code that sets self-sacrifice above all else.

The living, genuine ethos of symbiosis that East Asian people value is not restricted to, or defined by, distinctions posited by the "three relations," for example. It is a universal attitude, characterized by openness and dynamism, and it responds flexibly to changing times. As an ethos, it is distinct from both the non-being and primordial chaos of Taoist thought and from norms that constrain society and individuals.

The eminent French Sinologist Leon Vandermeersch made the far-seeing observation that

> Confucianism could not but disappear with the old society. . . . But precisely when Confucianism is completely dead can its legacy begin to be reinvested in new forms of thought without conflicting with the various factors of development.[2]

Perhaps "reinvestment" of the Confucian legacy can serve as an antidote to the excessive individualism of Western civilization and can help realize a universal "Way of Humanity." To find and follow a universal Way is one of the most important goals for civilization in the next century.

The ideal of *datong,* or "great unity," was a major concept in late Confucian thought in China, and it represented a step in the direction of an ethos of symbiosis. When Professor Kong Fan of this academy visited Japan in 1990, he gave a very enlightening presentation, in which he pointed out the deeply affirmative core of late Confucian philosophy. This is the philosophy of the great unity, which was articulated by Kang Youwei and Tan Sitong and was developed by Sun Wen (Sun Yat-sen). Tan Sitong brought out the purity and universality of the concept of great unity by describing it in a performative way. Throughout the realms of elements of existence, empty space, and sentient beings, it is something supremely refined and subtle. It makes everything adhere, penetrates everything, and connects everything so that all is permeated by it. The idea of great unity seems to me to be the dream of the Chinese people for an ideal society, a grand utopia, based on the ethos of symbiosis.

Rectification of Names

One of the sources of the utopian vision is the fierce, internal intellectual struggle of Confucius himself. Several famous passages from the *Analects* reveal the precise and balanced stance that Confucius took between human knowledge and actions, on the one hand, and transcendental wisdom, on the other:

> To say that you know when you do know and to say that you do not know when you do not know—that is knowledge. (*Analects* II, xvii)

> If we are not yet able to serve man, how can we serve spiritual beings? (*Analects* XI, xii)

If we do not know about life, how can we know about death? (*Analects* XI, xii)

These powerful declarations, which call to mind Socrates's "wisdom of ignorance," could only have come from a mind that was as formidable as it was humble. Confucius's conclusions are expressed as aphorisms, because their semantic import is visually clear and convincing in the medium of Chinese characters. However, the intellectual struggle that preceded the formation of these simple statements is analogous to the voluminous, penetrating dialogues and debates that Socrates engaged in, and that ultimately cost him his life.

Perhaps the archetypical expression of Confucius's intense soul-searching is the question posed by Zilu (Tzu-lu), which was to be pivotal in developing the theory of "the rectification of names":

Zilu said, "If the Lord of Wei left the administration of his state to you, what would you put first"?

The Master said, "If something has to be put first, it is, perhaps, the rectification of names."

Zilu said, "Is that so? What a roundabout way you take! Why bring rectification in at all?"

The Master said, "You, how boorish you are. Where a gentleman is ignorant, one would expect him not to offer any opinion. When names are not correct, what is said will not sound reasonable; when what is said does not sound reasonable, affairs will not culminate in success; when affairs do not culminate in success, rites and music will not flourish; when rites and music do not flourish, punishments will not fit the crimes; when punishments do not fit the crimes, the common people will not know where to put hand and foot. Thus when the gentleman names something, the name is sure to be usable in speech, and when he says something this is sure to be practicable. The thing about the gentleman is that he is anything but casual where speech is concerned." (*Analects* XIII, iii)

Here, the statement, "Where a gentleman is ignorant, one would expect him not to offer any opinion" corresponds to the passage quoted earlier: "To say that you know when you do know and to say that you do not know when you do not know - that is knowledge." The rigoristic, ascetic attitude toward language seems to be a feature common to all great minds, past and present. At issue is the correspondence of language to reality, or name to thing. In the Middle Ages, the European scholastic philosophers carried on a fruitless and seemingly endless debate concerning Realism and Nominalism. In periods of upheaval, as the general atmosphere of crisis grows, great thinkers often turn their attention to the redefinition of terminology. This was true of Socrates, and of Descartes, the "father of modern philosophy." Descartes lived during a time of chaos after the collapse of the scholastic hierarchy. Before he could arrive at the single declaration, "I think, therefore I am," he had to complete a pilgrimage of astonishing endurance and relentless self-examination.

We can see the same concern in the pained confession of Confucius, "I am thinking of giving up speech" (*Analects* XVII, xix) that so surprised his disciple, Zigong (Tzu-kung). Many centuries later, reflecting the sense of crisis that prevailed in late Qing China, Tan Sitong also protested that "names" were an obstacle to understanding humanity. In his writing he indicted the frailty of human judgment, preoccupied as it is with names. The vigorous renewal of interest in language today, in both West and East, points to the thick darkness that blankets these closing years of the twentieth century.

It is important to recognize the absolute radicalism of Confucius when, in seeking to harmonize rites, music, and punishments, the essential principles of government and basis of the social hierarchy, he makes the rectification of names the anchor of his policy. Certainly, his exchange with Zilu may have been a political argument about succession to the throne, a discussion of who calls himself ruler and who deserves to call himself ruler. However, the radical nature of his thought goes beyond its application in the political realm. In his attempt to unify language and reality, Confucius struggles toward a higher spiritual purity. His thought anticipates the search for the ultimate source of order, or the cosmic axis, as it is sometimes described.

From ancient times, those systems of thought that merit the name "philosophy" or "religion" have developed an all-embracing worldview with at least two dimensions. The first is a theory of value, or ethics, that relates to how human life should be lived. The second is a theory of being, or ontology, which posits the structure of existence, or of the world. It is often observed that the thought of Confucius, Mencius, and other early Confucian scholars was ontologically impoverished compared with its wealth of ethical content. Yet in the Master's statement, "If something has to be put first, it is, perhaps, the rectification of names," it is possible to detect a hint of the ontology of Song Confucianism, which later on developed into a sophisticated system enriched by Buddhism and other schools of thought.

The statement regarding the rectification of names condenses the pure centripetal force of hierarchy into the terse precision of words that declare the prophetic quality of their content. This may be the reason that the unique philosophy dealing with language and known as the rectification of names spread as widely as it did. Certainly, the influence of this philosophy went far beyond its time and place, exploding into the world of thought from a single remark giving priority to the "rectification of names."

Buddhism and Confucianism

Precipitous it may seem, but I would like to compare this remark of Confucius with that of the sixth-century Chinese Buddhist philospher Tiantai Zhiyi in *Hokke Gengi* (Profound Meaning of the Lotus Sutra): "At the beginning of the kalpa of continuance, the various things in the world had no names. The sage observed the principles that govern them and on that basis made up names for them."[3] While Confucius seeks order by rectifying names, Zhiyi speaks of creating names to produce order. Although the nuances may differ, both Confucianism and Chinese Buddhism play up the importance of *names,* the finishing stroke on the hierarchy woven and built by all existing things.

This emphasis has a very "Chinese" quality. Within the same broad tradition of Mahayana Buddhism, we find the Indian master Nagarjuna, in his *Chu Ron* (The Middle Doctrine), moving through the phenomenal world of discrimination and distinctions established by names, into a world of nondiscrimination and nondistinction. He focuses on the progression from earthly existence to a realm beyond. In contrast, Zhiyi, though he passes through the stage of release from the world into a realm that transcends it, returns to secular reality in the end. The vector from the earthly to transcendental existence is reversed. Although he seeks it in typical Buddhist fashion, Zhiyi develops the concept of universality in such a way that, unlike Nagarjuna, he finds it in the concrete world of phenomena. To me, Zhiyi's approach reveals the influence of East Asian spirituality. Professor Kong Fan identified the same influence in his lecture: Buddhist thought, he said, also sought the assistance of Confucianism, and in blending with Confucianism was able to develop within the context of Chinese society.

Zhiyi's reversal of the vector back to the concrete world does not represent a change in the nature of Buddhism. Rather, it speaks of the evolution of the religion that takes place in its transmission from one age to the next. It was precisely because Buddhist thought recognized the importance of the phenomenal world that it could imbibe and sublimate the ethos of symbiosis coursing through the underlayers of East Asian spirituality. Had Buddhism lacked the ability to adapt, it could never have achieved its central purpose, which is the salvation of all sentient beings.

In 1988, I met in Tokyo with a group of Chinese scholars headed by Liu Guoguang, the first vice-president of this Academy. At that time we talked about the writings of Tiantai Zhiyi and their basic premises. I stressed to the delegation that true Buddhism does not exist somewhere apart from this world of constant influx and change. Rather than being distinct from the chaos of the phenomenal realm, it is inseparably bound up in economics, politics, daily life, and culture. The great mission of Buddhism, moreover, is to provide energy to all aspects of human activity and channel them toward the realization of true value.

The words of Zhiyi quoted above are explained in the best tradition of Mahayana Buddhism as follows:

The supreme principle (which is the Mystic Law) was originally without a name. When the sage was observing the principle and assigning names to all things, he perceived that there
is this wonderful single Law which simultaneously possesses
both cause and effect, and he named it *Myoho-renge* [Literally,
"Lotus of the Mystic Law"]. This single Law encompasses
within it all the laws or phenomena comprising the Ten
Worlds and the three thousand realms, and is lacking in none
of them. Anyone who practices this Law will obtain both the
cause and the effect of Buddhahood simultaneously.[4]

The first part of the commentary refers to the *Hokke gengi* and
discusses the creation of names, while the second section is a sum-
mary of Zhiyi's ontology of *ichinen sanzen* (a single life-moment
possesses three thousand realms). It reads: "This single Law which is
Myoho-renge encompasses within it all the laws or phenomena comprising the Ten Worlds and the three thousand realms, and is lacking
in none of them." The final sentence, "Anyone who practices this
Law will obtain both the cause and the effect of Buddhahood
simultaneously," refers, of course, to the criteria by which we should
live our lives. It thus represents a theory of both value and practice.
The strong implications of social activity in the commentary partly
compensate for a shortcoming of Tiantai Buddhism, which was the
lack of the practicality necessary to be called an ethos. The commentary, however, is a bold and definitive articulation of a religious
worldview that incorporates ontology and ethics.

Zhou Enlai

The ethos of symbiosis, an enduring and valuable expression of East
Asian spirituality, has persisted as an underground stream for several
millennia. During that time it has contributed a unique humanitarian element to many later developments, including Chinese socialism. There is not space here to pursue that point very far, but I
would like to consider the character of the late Premier Zhou Enlai,
who I believe personified a life lived by the ethos of symbiosis.

I met the premier once, about a year before he died. And recently I had a talk with Han Xu, president of the Chinese People's Association for Friendship with Foreign Countries, who worked with Zhou Enlai for a number of years at the Ministry of Foreign Affairs. The many anecdotes that Han Xu shared with me only increased my respect for Zhou, a remarkable man. Zhou Enlai's concern for the foreign guests he entertained and his attentiveness to their well-being were extraordinary. The premier had astonishing powers of memory, developed out of an intense, earnest sense of duty. This tireless man's sense of responsibility seemed to extend not only to China but to the world itself.

Premier Zhou Enlai had character that befitted his role. He was fair and even-handed, never allowing relatives or close associates to use his name or influence for their own benefit. He always saw the large picture, yet he did not overlook the details. Retaining a firm conviction in his heart, he presented a gentle smile to the world. He was not self-centered but other-centered, and was both a model Chinese and supremely cosmopolitan. With his affectionate gaze directed toward the people of his nation, he was a magnificent soul, heir to the spirit of the early-twentieth-century writer Lü Xun (1881–1936), who declared "The revolution must give people life, not take it from them." Zhou was the rare, living and breathing embodiment of the ethos of symbiosis, favoring harmony over opposition, unity over division, "we" over "I." In these last years of our century, when human relations are so deeply troubled, he was a man with the kind of character that we urgently need.

The ethos of symbiosis is not bound to the realm of human society alone. It is cosmic, working throughout nature and the universe. The Buddhist belief in the interrelatedness of humanity and nature is expressed by the dictum that "mountains and rivers, grasses and trees all attain Buddhahood." This spiritual conviction will play an ever more important role as the problems of environmental pollution and destruction, and of dwindling resources grow increasingly serious. As the twenty-first century dawns, the world will keep its attention not just on the economic performance of East Asia, but on the depth of its spirituality as well. The region will become a driving force in history, a source of new hope and expectation for all people.

Allow me to close by quoting a stanza by the fourth-century poet Tao Qian:

> Why must friends all be old time associates?
> With even a casual acquaintance one may speak frank words.
> This visitor of mine approves my tastes;
> again and again he comes to peer into my garden.
> Our talks are pleasant, free from all vulgarity;
> we speak of the writings of the sages.

NOTES

1. The three relations are between ruler and minister, between father and son, and between husband and wife. The five practices are humanity, righteousness, rites, wisdom, and faith.

2. Leon Vandermeersch, *Ajia Bunka-ken no Jidai,* trans. Tadayuki Fukukane (Tokyo: Taishukan Shoten, Ltd.1987), 184.

3. Gosho Translation Committee, trans. and ed., *The Major Writings of Nichiren Daishonin* (Tokyo: NSIC, 1994), 7:64.

4. Ibid., 65–66.

Mahayana Buddhism
and Twenty-first-Century Civilization

A speech delivered at Harvard University, Cambridge,
September 24, 1993

Nothing could please me more than to be back at Harvard University, to speak with faculty and students at this time-honored institution of unexcelled academic endeavor. To Professor Nur Yalman, Professor Harvey Cox, Professor John Kenneth Galbraith, and all the others who have made my visit possible, I extend grateful thanks.

The Continuity of Life and Death

It was the Greek philosopher Heraclitus who declared that all things are in a state of flux and that change is the essential nature of reality. Indeed, everything, whether it lies in the realm of natural phenomena or of human affairs, changes continuously. Nothing maintains exactly the same state for even the briefest instant; the most solid-seeming rocks and minerals are subject to the erosive effects of time. But during this century of war and revolution, normal change and flux seem to have been accelerated and magnified. We have seen the most extraordinary panorama of social transformations.

The Buddhist term for the ephemeral aspect of reality is "the transience of all phenomena" (*shogyo mujo* in Japanese). In the Bud-

151

dhist cosmology, this concept is described as the repeated cycles of formation, continuance, decline, and disintegration through which all systems must pass. During our lives as human beings, we experience transience as the four sufferings: the suffering of birth (and of day-to-day existence), that of illness, of aging, and finally, of death. No human being is exempt from these sources of pain. It was, in fact, human distress, in particular the problem of death, that spawned the formation of religious and philosophical systems. It is said that Shakyamuni was inspired to seek the truth by his accidental encounters with many sorrows at the gates of the palace in which he was raised. Plato stated that true philosophers are always engaged in the practice of dying, while Nichiren, founder of the school of Buddhism followed by members of Soka Gakkai International, admonishes us to "first study death, then study other matters."[1]

Death weighs heavily on the human heart as an inescapable reminder of the finite nature of our existence. However seemingly limitless the wealth or power we might attain, the reality of our eventual demise cannot be avoided. From ancient times, humanity has sought to conquer the fear and apprehension surrounding death by finding ways to partake of the eternal. Through this quest, people have learned to overcome control by instinctual modes of survival and have developed the characteristics that we recognize as uniquely human. In that perspective, we can see why the history of religion coincides with the history of humankind.

Modern civilization has attempted to ignore death. We have diverted our gaze from this most fundamental of concerns as we try to drive death into the shadows. For many people living today, death is the mere absence of life; it is blankness; it is the void. Life is identified with all that is good: with being, rationality, and light. In contrast, death is perceived as evil, as nothingness, and as the dark and irrational. Only the negative perception of death prevails.

We cannot, however, ignore death, and the attempt to do so has exacted a heavy price. The horrific and ironic climax of modern civilization has been in our time what Zbigniew Brzezinski has called the "century of megadeath." Today, a wide range of issues is now forcing a reexamination and reevaluation of the significance of death. They include questions about brain death and death with dignity, the function of hospices, alternative funerary styles and rites, and research into death and dying by writers such as Elisabeth Kubler-Ross.

We finally seem to be ready to recognize the fundamental error in our view of life and death. We are beginning to understand that death is more than the absence of life; that death, together with active life, is necessary for the formation of a larger, more essential, whole. This greater whole reflects the deeper continuity of life and death that we experience as individuals and express as culture. A central challenge for the coming century will be to establish a culture based on an understanding of the relationship of life and death and of life's essential eternity. Such an attitude does not disown death, but directly confronts and correctly positions it within the larger context of life.

Buddhism speaks of an intrinsic nature (*hossho* in Japanese, sometimes translated as "Dharma nature") existing within the depths of phenomenal reality. This nature depends upon and responds to environmental conditions, and it alternates between states of emergence and latency. All phenomena, including life and death, can be seen as elements within the cycle of emergence and latency, or manifestation and withdrawal.

Cycles of life and death can be likened to the alternating periods of sleep and wakefulness. Just as sleep prepares us for the next day's activity, death can be seen as a state in which we rest and replenish ourselves for new life. In this light, death should be acknowledged, along with life, as a blessing to be appreciated. The Lotus Sutra, the core of Mahayana Buddhism, states that the purpose of existence, the eternal cycles of life and death, is to be "happy and at ease." It further teaches that sustained faith and practice enable us to know a deep and abiding joy in death as well as in life, to be equally "happy and at ease"[2] with both. Nichiren describes the attainment of this state as the "greatest of all joys."[3]

If the tragedies of this century of war and revolution have taught us anything, it is the folly of believing that reform of external factors, such as social systems, is the linchpin to achieving happiness. I am convinced that in the coming century, the greatest emphasis must be placed on fostering inwardly-directed change. In addition, our efforts must be inspired by a new understanding of life and death.

There are three broad areas where Mahayana Buddhism can help solve the problems suggested above, and make a positive difference to civilization in the twenty-first century. Let us consider those aspects of Buddhism that offer workable, constructive guidance.

The Buddhist Emphasis on Dialogue

Since its inception, the philosophy of Buddhism has been associated with peace and pacifism. That emphasis derives principally from the consistent rejection of violence combined with stress on dialogue and discussion as the best means of resolving conflict. Descriptions of the life of Shakyamuni provide a good illustration. His life was completely untrammeled by dogma, and his interactions with his fellows stressed the importance of dialogue. The sutra recounting the travels that culminated his Buddhist practice begins with an episode in which the aged Shakyamuni uses the power of language to avert an invasion.[4]

According to the sutra, Shakyamuni, then eighty years old, did not directly admonish the minister of Magadha, a large country bent on conquering the neighboring state of Vajji. Instead, he spoke persuasively about the principles by which nations prosper and decline. His discourse dissuaded the minister from implementing the planned attack. The final chapter of the same sutra concludes with a moving description of Shakyamuni on his deathbed. As he lay dying, he repeatedly urged his disciples to raise any uncertainties that they might have about the Buddhist Law (Dharma) or its practice, so that they would not find themselves regretting unasked questions after his passing. Up until his last moment, Shakyamuni actively sought out dialogue, and the drama of his final voyage from beginning to end is illuminated by the light of language, skillfully wielded by one who was truly a "master of words."

Why was Shakyamuni able to employ language with such freedom and to such effect? What made him such a peerless master of dialogue? I believe that his fluency was due to the expansiveness of his enlightened state, utterly free of all dogma, prejudice, and attachment. The following quote is illustrative: "I perceived a single, invisible arrow piercing the hearts of the people."[5] The "arrow" symbolizes a prejudicial mindset, an unreasoning emphasis on individual differences. India at that time was going through transition and upheaval, and the horrors of conflict and war were an ever-present reality. To Shakyamuni's penetrating gaze, it was clear that the underlying cause of the conflict was attachment to distinctions, to ethnic, national, and other differences.

In the early years of this century, Josiah Royce (one of many important philosophers Harvard University has given the world) declared that:

Reform, in such matters, must come, if at all, from within. . . .
The public as a whole is whatever the processes that occur, for good or evil, in individual minds, may determine.[6]

As Royce points out, the "invisible arrow" of evil is not to be found in the existence of races and classes external to ourselves, but is embedded in our own hearts. The conquest of our own prejudicial thinking, our own attachment to difference, is the necessary precondition for open dialogue. Such discussion, in turn, is essential for the establishment of peace and universal respect for human rights. It was his own complete absence of prejudice that enabled Shakyamuni to expound the Law with such freedom, adapting his style of teaching to the character and capacity of the person to whom he was speaking.

Whether he was mediating a communal dispute over water rights, converting a violent criminal, or admonishing someone who objected to the practice of begging, Shakyamuni attempted first to make others aware of the "arrow" of their inner evil. The power of his extraordinary character brought these words to the lips of one contemporaneous sovereign: "Those whom we, with weapons, cannot force to surrender, you subdue unarmed."[7]

Only by overcoming attachment to differences can a religion rise above an essentially tribal outlook to offer a global faith. Nichiren, for example, dismissed the shogunal authorities, who were persecuting him, as the "rulers of this little island country."[8] His vision was broader, directed toward establishing a religious spirit that would embody universal values and transcend the confines of a single state.

Dialogue is not limited to formal debate or placid exchange that wafts by like a spring breeze. There are times when, to break the grip of arrogance, speech must be like the breath of fire. Thus, although we typically associate Shakyamuni and Nagarjuna only with mildness, it was the occasional ferocity of their speech that earned them the sobriquet of "those who deny everything"[9] in their respective eras.

Similarly, Nichiren, who demonstrated a familial affection and tender concern for the common people, was uncompromising in his confrontations with corrupt and degenerate authority. Always unarmed in the chronically violent Japan of his time, he relied exclusively and unflinchingly on the power of persuasion and nonviolence. He was tempted with the promise of absolute power if he renounced his faith, and threatened with the beheading of his parents if he adhered to his beliefs. Nevertheless, he maintained the courage of his convictions. The following passage, written upon his exile to a distant island from which none was expected to return, typifies his lionesque tone: "Whatever obstacles I might encounter, so long as men of wisdom do not prove my teachings to be false, I will never yield!"[10]

Nichiren's faith in the power of language was absolute. If more people were to pursue dialogue in an equally unrelenting manner, the inevitable conflicts of human life would surely find easier resolution. Prejudice would yield to empathy and war would give way to peace. Genuine dialogue results in the transformation of opposing viewpoints, changing them from wedges that drive people apart into bridges that link them together.

During World War II, Soka Gakkai, an organization based on the teachings of Nichiren, challenged head-on the forces of Japanese militarism. As a result, many members were imprisoned, beginning with the founder and first president Tsunesaburo Makiguchi. Far from recanting, Makiguchi continued to explain to his guards and interrogators the principles of Buddhism. They were the very ideas which had made him a "thought criminal" in the first place. He died at the age of seventy-three, still in confinement.

Josei Toda was heir to the spiritual legacy of Makiguchi, and he became the second president of the organization. He emerged from the ordeal of two years' imprisonment declaring his faith in the unity of the global human family. He then preached widely among the population, who were lost and suffering in the aftermath of the war. Toda also bequeathed to us, his youthful disciples, the mission of building a world free of nuclear weapons.

With this as our historical and philosophical basis, Soka Gakkai International remains committed to the role of dialogue in the advancement of peace, education, and culture. At present, we are engaged in forging bonds of solidarity with citizens in one hundred fifteen countries and regions around the world. For my own part, I wish only to continue my efforts to speak with people all over the earth in order to contribute in some small way to the greater happiness of humankind.

Restoring Humanity

What role can Buddhism play in the restoration and rejuvenation of humanity? In an age marked by widespread religious revival, we need always ask: Does religion make people stronger, or weaker? Does it encourage what is good or what is evil in them? Are they made better and wiser by religion? While the authority of Marx as social prophet has been largely undermined by the collapse of socialism in Eastern Europe and the former Soviet Union, there is an important truth contained in his description of religion as the "opiate of the masses." In fact, there is reason for concern that more than a few of the religions finding new life in the twilight of this century are characterized by dogmatism and insularity, traits that run counter to the accelerating trend toward interdependence and cross-cultural interaction.

With this in mind, let us examine the relative weight that different belief systems assign to self-reliance, as opposed to dependence on powers external to the self. These two tendencies correspond roughly to the Christian concepts of free will and grace.

Broadly speaking, the passage from medieval to modern Europe coincided with a steady movement away from a theistic determinism, toward ever-greater emphasis on free will and human responsibility. Human abilities were encouraged, and reliance on external, abstract authority declined, making way for the great achievements of science and technology. More and more people began to believe in the omnipotence of reason and its scientific fruits. But to be blindly convinced of the power of technology can lead to the hubris of assuming that there is nothing we are unable to accomplish. It may be true that dependence on some external authority led people to underestimate both our potential and our responsibility, but excessive faith in our own powers is not the answer; it has, in fact, produced a dangerous overconfidence in ourselves.

We are now seeking a third path, a new balance between faith in ourselves and recognition of a power that is greater than we are. These words of Nichiren illustrate the subtle and richly suggestive Mahayana perspective on attaining enlightenment: "Neither solely through one's own efforts . . . nor solely through the power of others."[11] The persuasive argument of Buddhism is its conviction that the greatest good is derived from the dynamic fusion and balancing of internal and external forces.

Similarly, John Dewey, in *A Common Faith,* asserts that it is "the religious," rather than specific religions, that is of vital importance. While religions all too quickly fall into dogmatism and fanaticism, "that which is religious" has the power to "unify interests and energies" and to "direct action and generate the heat of emotion and the light of intelligence." Likewise, "the religious" enables the realization of those benefits that Dewey identifies as "the values of art in all its forms, of knowledge, of effort, and of rest after striving, of education and fellowship, of friendship and love, of growth in mind and body."[12]

Dewey does not identify a specific external power. For him "the religious" is a generalized term for that which supports and encourages people in the active pursuit of the good and the valuable. "The religious," as he defines it, helps those who help themselves.

As Dewey understood, and as the sad outcome of people's self-worship in modern times has demonstrated, without assistance we are incapable of living up to our potential. Only by relying on and merging with the eternal can we fully activate all our capabilities. Thus, we need help, but our human potential does not come from outside; it is, and always has been, of us and within us. How any given religious tradition handles the balance between interior and exterior forces will, I believe, decisively affect its long-term viability.

Anyone involved in religion must constantly work on keeping the balance, if we do not want to repeat history. For if we are not attentive, religion can enslave us to dogma and to its own authority just as easily as the religious impulse can serve as a vehicle for human restoration and rejuvenation.

Perhaps because our Buddhist movement is so human-centered, Harvey Cox of the Harvard Divinity School has described it as an effort to define the humanistic direction of religion. Indeed, Buddhism is not merely a theoretical construct; it helps us steer our lives, as we actually live them, moment by moment, toward the achievement of happiness and worth. Thus, Nichiren states:

> When you concentrate the exertions of one hundred million aeons in a single life-moment, the three inherent properties of the Buddha will become manifest in your every thought and act.[13]

The expression "exertions of one hundred million aeons" refers to the ability to confront each of life's problems with our full being, awakening the total consciousness, leaving no inner resource untapped. By wholeheartedly and directly meeting the challenges of life, we bring forth from within ourselves the "three inherent properties of the Buddha." It is the light of this internal wisdom that constantly encourages and guides us toward true and correct action.

The vibrant tones of the drums, horns, and other musical instruments that appear throughout the Lotus Sutra work metaphorically to encourage the human will to live. The function of the Buddha nature is always to urge us to be strong, good, and wise. The message of the sutra is one of human restoration.

The Interrelationship of All Things

Buddhism provides a philosophical basis for the symbiotic coexistence of all things. Among the many images in the Lotus Sutra, a particularly compelling one is the merciful rain that falls everywhere, equally, moistening the vast expanse of the earth and bringing forth new life from all the trees and grasses, large and small. This scene, depicted with the vividness, grandeur, and beauty characteristic of the Lotus Sutra, symbolizes the enlightenment of all people touched by the Buddha's Law. At the same time, it is a magnificent tribute to the rich diversity of human and all other forms of sentient and non-sentient life. Thus, each living thing manifests the enlightenment of which it is capable; each contributes to the harmony of the grand concert of symbiosis. In Buddhist terminology, "dependent origination" (*engi*) describes these relationships. Nothing and nobody exists in isolation. Each individual being functions to create the environment that sustains all other existences. All things are mutually supporting and interrelated, forming a living cosmos, what modern philosophy might term a semantic whole. That is the conceptual framework through which Mahayana Buddhism views the natural universe.

Speaking through Faust, Goethe gives voice to a similar vision. "Into the whole, how all things blend, each in the other working, living."[14] These lines are striking for their remarkable affinity with Buddhist thought.. Although Johann Peter Eckermann criticized Goethe for "lacking confirmation of his presentiments,"[15] the intervening years have seen a steadily swelling affirmation of the deductive vision in both Goethe and Buddhist thought.

Consider, for example, the concept of causation. When viewed in terms of dependent origination, causal relationships differ fundamentally from the mechanistic idea of cause and effect that, according to modern science, holds sway over the objective natural world. In the scientific model, reality is divorced from subjective human concerns. When an accident or disaster takes place, for example, a mechanistic theory of causation can be used to pursue and identify how the accident occurred. It is silent, however, on other points, including the question of why certain individuals and not others should find themselves caught up in the tragic event. Indeed, the mechanistic view of nature requires the deliberate dismissal of existential questions.

In contrast, the Buddhist understanding of causation is more broadly defined and takes account of human existence. It seeks to directly address these poignant uncertainties, as in the following exchange that occurred early in Shakyamuni's career: "What is the cause of aging and death? Birth is the cause of aging and death."[16]

In a later era, through a process of exhaustive personal inquiry, Zhiyi, the founder of the Chinese Tiantai school of Buddhism, developed a theoretical structure that included such concepts as the "three thousand realms in a single life-moment." It is not only sweeping in scope and rigorous in elaboration, but is entirely compatible with modern science. While limitations of time prohibit discussion of his system, it is worth mentioning that many contemporary fields of inquiry—for example, ecology, transpersonal psychology, and quantum mechanics—have some interesting points in common with Buddhism in their approach and conclusions.

The Buddhist emphasis on relatedness and interdependence may seem to suggest that individual identity is obscured. Buddhist scripture addresses this in the following passage:

You are your own master. Could anyone else be your master? When you have gained control over yourself, you have found a master of rare value.[17]

A second passage reads:

Be lamps unto yourselves. Rely on yourselves. Hold fast to the Law as a lamp, do not rely on anything else.[18]

Both passages urge us to live independently, true to ourselves and unswayed by others. The "self" referred to here, however, is not the Buddhist "lesser self" (*shoga*), caught up in the snares of egoism. Rather, it is the "greater self" (*taiga*), fused with the life of the universe through which cause and effect intertwine over the infinite reaches of space and time.

The greater, cosmic self is related to the unifying and integrating "self" that Jung perceived in the depths of the ego. It is also similar to Ralph Waldo Emerson's "The universal beauty, to which every part and particle is equally related; the eternal One."[19]

I am firmly convinced that a large-scale awakening to the greater self will lead to a world of creative coexistence in the coming century. Recall the lines of Walt Whitman, in which he sings the praises of the human spirit:

But that I,
turning to thee O soul,
thou actual Me,
And lo,
thou gently masterest the orbs,
Thou matest Time,
smilest content at Death,
And fillest,
swellest full the vastness of space.[20]

The greater self of Mahayana Buddhism is another way of expressing the openness and expansiveness of character that embraces the sufferings of all people as one's own. This self always seeks ways of alleviating the pain and augmenting the happiness of others, here, amid the realities of everyday life. Only the solidarity brought about by such natural human nobility will break down the isolation of the modern self and lead to the dawning of new hope for civilization. Furthermore, it is the dynamic, vital awakening of the greater self that will enable each of us, as individuals, to experience both life and death with equal delight. Thus, as Nichiren stated: "We adorn the treasure tower of our being with the four aspects [of birth, aging, sickness, and death]."[21]

It is my earnest desire and prayer that in the twenty-first century each member of the human family will let shine the natural luster of their inner "treasure tower." Filling our azure planet with the chorus of open dialogue, humankind will move on into the new millennium.

NOTES

1. Nichiko Hori, ed., *Nichiren Daishonin Gosho Zenshu* (Tokyo: Soka Gakkai, 1952), 1404.

2. J. Takakusu, ed., *Taisho Issaikyo* (Tokyo: Taisho Issaikyo Publishing Society, 1925), vol.9, 43c.

3. Hori, 788.

4. J. Takakusu, ed., *Nanden Daizokyo.* (Tokyo: Taisho Shinshu Daizokyo Publishing Society, 1935), vol.7, 27ff.

5. J. Takakusu, ed., *Nanden Daizokyo*, vol.24, p.358.

6. Josiah Royce, *The Basic Writings of Josiah Royce* (Chicago: The University of Chicago Press, 1969), 2:1122.

7. J. Takakusu, ed., *Nanden Daizokyo*, vol.11a, 137.

8. Philip B, Yampolsky, *Selected Writings of Nichiren,* trans. Burton Watson (New York: Columbia University Press, 1990), 322.

9. J. Takakusu, ed., *Taisho Issaikyo*, vol.30.

10. Yampolsky, 138.

11. Hori, 403.

12. John Dewey, *A Common Faith* (New Haven: Yale University Press, 1934), 50-52.

13. Hori, 790.

14. J. W. Goethe, *Faust A Tragedy,* trans. Bayard Taylor (New York: The Modern Library, 1967), 17–18.

15. Johann Wolfgang von Goethe, *Conversations of Goethe with Eckermann* (London: J. M. Dent and Sons Ltd., 1930), 101.

16. J. Takakusu, ed., *Nanden Daizokyo*, vol. 13, 1ff.

17. J. Takakusu, ed., *Nanden Daizokyo*, vol.23, p.42.

18. J. Takakusu, ed., *Taisho Issaikyo*, vol.1, 645c, 15b.

19. Ralph Waldo Emerson, *Essays and Poems of Emerson* (New York: Harcourt, Brace and Company, 1921), 45.

20. Walt Whitman, *Leaves of Grass* (Garden City: Doubleday & Company, 1926), 348.

21. Hori, 740.

PART IV

The Imperative of Peace

Radicalism Reconsidered

A speech delivered at Claremont McKenna College,
Claremont, California, January 29, 1993

It is with a feeling of exuberance that I join you today, sensing the vigor, energy, and intellectual vitality of Claremont McKenna College. I am honored to have been invited to speak, and I extend my greetings and grateful thanks to President Jack L. Stark, the members of the faculty, and students.

New Principles of Integration

Only a few years remain before we begin the twenty-first century, and our world seems to slide deeper into the malaise and disorder so often associated with *fin-de-siècle*. Among its constant features, history has demonstrated cycles of coming together and breaking apart, integration and disintegration, but now we face the prospect of pitching into a level of global chaos from which there may be no recovery. I refer to the extremely potent disintegrative forces of national and ethnic "fundamentalism," which, in the wake of the Cold War, are emerging to fill the vacuum left by the abandonment of ideology as the ersatz principle around which our world was ordered and integrated.

At each important juncture in recent history—the liberation of Eastern Europe, the peaceful birth of a reunified Germany, and the end of the Gulf War—we have heard discussions of the need for a vision on which to base a new international order. But dreams have rapidly faded, and still we are searching blindly for the outlines, having achieved only a general agreement that whatever form a new order takes, the United Nations will play a central role.

Our world can be likened to the burnt crust that is left after an all-consuming conflagration. If we are to sow this desolate bed with the seeds for new growth, we cannot depend on the old guidelines. We must put our full energies into the task of discovering new principles of integration for our world.

Peoples and nations have only just begun to awaken from their long intoxication with ideology. Several of my friends from the former Soviet Union have used the parable of Procrustes's bed to describe the domination and victimization of people by ideology.[1] When we pause to think of the enormous sacrifice and the toll of human suffering that have been the price of attachment to ideology, it is clear that the search for integrating principles must be conducted with great caution. That search cannot be transcendent but must be entirely human in scale, directed at our inner life. For the essence of our quest is the recovery and revival of the totality and unity of human experience that is being so disastrously eroded by accelerating fragmentation.

In an interview published in the Soka Gakkai's daily newspaper, the *Seikyo Shimbun,* pioneer researcher in psycho-pharmacology Dr. Joel Elkes astutely observed: "Healing is a restoration to the whole. . . . The words 'healing', 'whole' and 'holy' all derive from the same root. To be holy is to be complete, connected as a person and with other persons, connected with the planet. Pain is a signal that the part has become loose from the whole."[2] This observation applies not just to physiological pain, but to all that ails our contemporary civilization, whose fundamental pathogenesis can be found in the breakdown of human wholeness.

It has been some time since expressions such as "the totality of humanity" have ceased to summon a vivid image to our minds.

Human wholeness might be conceived as a generic term embracing our potential for wisdom (*homo sapiens*), our entrepreneurial skills (*homo economicus*), our ability to work transformations (*homo faber*), or our playfulness (*homo ludens*). But this is little more than an array of definitions and as such is too simplistic to capture the essence of human wholeness.

Start With the Sun

In the final chapter of his admonitory work *Apocalypse,* D. H. Lawrence repeats his frequent appeal for a restoration of wholeness, delineating the problem with great clarity:

> What man most passionately wants is his living wholeness and his living unison, not his own isolated salvation of his "soul"....
> What we want is to destroy our false, inorganic connections, especially those related to money, and re-establish the living organic connections, with the cosmos, the sun and earth, with mankind and nation and family. Start with the sun, and the rest will slowly, slowly happen.[3]

What Lawrence expresses with such poetry has a remarkable parallel in the words of Eduard Heimann, whose macroscopic analyses of social dynamics have invited comparison with Marx and Schumpeter. Heimann advances the idea that the term "organic growth" can be applied to those modalities of social development in which the wholeness of the human person and the unity of life are left intact. "If we may be permitted for present purposes the use of a dangerous analogy, 'the organism' of society lives and evolves, growing and changing while maintaining its identity."[4] Needless to say, modern society has drifted far from any semblance of healthy, ideal "organic growth."

Human wholeness refers to that vibrant state of being where we can absorb and embody the immanent rhythms of cosmic life in new patterns of action and activity, and in so doing, give vital meaning to history and traditions. The experience of human wholeness is one of deep fulfillment, enabling us to manifest the qualities—such as composure and generosity, tolerance and consideration—that have been considered virtues since ancient times. Conversely, people who sever themselves from history and tradition, from others and the cosmos, are fated to an uncontrollable process of degeneration and loss of self, leading to nervous torment, instability and, finally, madness.

It is sometimes suggested nowadays that Nietzsche's "last man" is the image of modern humanity, yet the very idea itself is but another aspect of instability and loss of self. The "last man" is anything but history's victor. He seems inescapably trapped within the "false, inorganic connections, especially those related to money," of which Lawrence warns. If this is the contemporary *homo economicus,* what a long and sad decline from the independence and dynamism of the original economic man portrayed by Adam Smith! The transformation in this single aspect conveys incontrovertible evidence of human wholeness sundered, as we advance into modernity.

How can we restore wholeness to the human condition without jeopardizing the benefits of modernization, among them the work being done to eliminate hunger and disease? It is my belief that balanced, steady gradualism will allow us to rein in the terrible momentum of disintegration and develop new principles of integration. Such an approach may strike some as circuitous, but in the long run it represents the most direct and fundamental way to provide lasting solutions for the ills of our age. As we take on the challenge of this daunting task, there are a number of points to consider, the first of which is the importance of the gradualist approach to change.

Case for Gradualism

The year before last, the seventy-year experiment of communism in the Soviet Union culminated in abject failure. Some observers remarked that the Russians had ended the process started by the French Revolution. In other words, the dissolution of the Soviet Union thoroughly undercut attempts to view history as a linear, causal process in which, for example, the bourgeois revolution in

France must inevitably lead to a proletarian revolution in Russia. To me, such a diagnosis of the failure of what might be called the "radical rationalist approach to history" is convincing.

The historiographical premise behind that approach is the *a priori* existence of a blueprint for the rational development and advancement of history; it is a method that judges and seeks to remake reality against a single theoretical model. This approach reflects the unquestioning faith in reason that swept through nineteenth-century intellectual history. As it relates to the question of human wholeness, it exalts the single faculty of reason to the exclusion of all others. It was this mistaken sense of having mastered immutable laws of history that produced the repulsive intolerance and heady arrogance characteristic of so many modern revolutionaries. The sad irony is that most of them were originally motivated by good intentions.

There is a natural relation between rationalism and radicalism. If all events can be understood by rational processes, from which the blueprints for a rationalist utopia can be drawn, theoretically they can be speeded up, and the sooner the utopia is realized, the better. Equally "natural" is the quick resort to force in dealing with counterrevolutionary elements who refuse to adopt this utopian vision as their own.

This kind of radicalism does not necessarily have general appeal. Consider, for example, the words of the Kyrgyzstan-born novelist Chingiz Aitmatov, one of the leading lights of contemporary Russian literature. In the introduction to the volume containing the dialogue he and I have carried on over the past several years, Aitmatov has written:

Second, some fatherly advice: Young people, do not put your faith in social revolutions. For a nation, a people, and a society, revolution is riot, mass disease, mass violence, and general catastrophe. We have found that out to the fullest. Seek ways of democratic reform, like bloodless evolution and the sequential transformation of society. Evolution demands more time, patience, and compromise. It is the organization and augmentation of happiness, not its forceful establishment. I pray to God that the younger generations will learn from our mistakes.[5]

Interestingly, Aitmatov's trenchant critique of revolutionary radicalism echoes the charges Edmund Burke and Goethe leveled at Jacobinism.

Not only revolutionary radicalism but any worldview that bases itself on "historical inevitability" fundamentally denies the human capacity to create our own destiny through our own efforts. We must always resist the temptation to treat individual lives or history as mere objective things or facts; their truth can only be known through active, living engagement and participation. To be of real and lasting value, change must be gradual and inspired from within. The application of external, coercive force will always destroy some aspect of our total humanity and compromise the balance and integrity of life.

In this regard, there is considerable validity in the economist Friedrich A. Hayek's analogy of a gardener to describe the attitude a true liberal takes toward society. The growth of plant life is both spontaneous and gradual. At most, the gardener can create conditions propitious to growth. In the same way, Hayek urges, we must utilize the "spontaneous forces of society."[6]

Coincidentally, the gardener analogy also leads us to consider the need to respect diversity within society. One of the most critical questions today is how, after the fashion of a skilled gardener, we can create a harmonious garden from the manifold human talents and qualities, while respecting the unique and sacrosanct individuality of each person. By adopting an inner-directed and gradualist approach, we can find ways through which the diversity of our experience can become a source of creative energy. The tradition and experience of Americans, I believe, qualify the United States to assume a special mission to demonstrate a pattern for the entire world.

Let me also stress that just as radicalism is fated by its nature to resort to violence and terror, the most potent weapon in the arsenal of the gradualist is dialogue. In Socrates we see the steadfast commitment to dialogue, to verbal combat from which there is no retreat, and an intensity that is, in some literal sense, "death-defying." Such dialogue can only be sustained by resources of spiritual energy and strength far greater and deeper than will be found among those who so quickly turn to violence.

Discipline and Dialogue

It is only within the open space created by dialogue—whether conducted with our neighbors, with history, with nature, or the cosmos—that human wholeness can be sustained. The closed silence of an autistic space can only become the site of spiritual suicide. We are not born human in any but a biological sense; we can only learn to know ourselves and others and thus be "trained" in the ways of being human. We do this by immersion in the "ocean of language and dialogue" fed by the springs of cultural tradition.

I am reminded of the beautiful and moving passage in *Phaedo* in which Socrates teaches his youthful disciples that hatred of language and ideas (*misologos*) leads to antipathy toward humanity (*misanthropos*).[7] The mistrust of language that gives birth to a misologist is but the inverse of an excessive belief in the power of language. The two are different aspects of the same thing, which is a frailty of spirit unable to cope with the stresses of human proximity brought about by dialogue. Such spiritual weakness causes a person to vacillate between undue trustfulness and suspicion of other people, thus becoming easy prey for the forces of disintegration.

To be worthy of the name "dialogue," our efforts for dialogue's sake must be carried through to the end. To refuse peaceful exchange and choose force is to compromise and give in to human weakness; it is to admit the defeat of the human spirit. Socrates encourages his youthful disciples to train and strengthen themselves spiritually, to maintain hope and self-control, to advance courageously choosing virtue over material wealth, truth over fame.

While we cannot regard modern mass society in terms of the values of ancient Greece, we must not overemphasize the differences between them. In his classic study *Public Opinion,* Walter Lippmann, for one, repeatedly calls for Socratic dialogue and Socratic individuals as the keys to the more wholesome formation of public opinion.[8] When I recently met in Tokyo with President Jack L. Stark and Professor Alfred Balitzer of Claremont McKenna College, we all agreed fully on the primacy of education among social values. Education, based on open dialogue, is far more than the mere transfer of information and knowledge; it enables us to rise above the confines of our parochial perspectives and passions. Institutes of higher learning are charged with the task of encouraging Socratic world citizens and spearheading the search for new principles for the peaceful integration of our world.

Incidentally, Shakyamuni, who is often mentioned with Socrates as one of the world's great teachers, spent the last moments of his life exhorting his grieving disciples to engage him in dialogue. To the very end he, also, continued to urge them to question him on any subject, as one friend to another.

Character and Human Wholeness

My final point is the central importance of character, another name for human wholeness or completeness. The integrating principles to which I have been referring are not just abstractions, but something that must be sought inwardly by people striving to grow in character. It is character that, in the end, holds together the web of integrating forces.

Almost contemporaneous with the establishment of Claremont McKenna College, my mentor in life and second president of Soka Gakkai, Josei Toda, emerged from a two-year imprisonment by the forces of Japanese militarism, to initiate a new humanistic movement in Japan. In his efforts he always focused on raising people of character, one person at a time, from among the populace. I have many fond memories of this compassionate man, whose love for youth knew no bounds and who encouraged us to be great actors on the stage of life. Indeed, the power of character is like the concentrated energy of an actor who has given himself or herself entirely over to the performance of the part. A person of outstanding character will always, even under the most difficult circumstances, retain an air of composure, ease, and even humor, like an accomplished actor playing a part. This is nothing other than the achievement of self-mastery or self-control.

Goethe, who was an outstanding stage director in addition to his other talents, responded when asked what he looked for in an actor:

[A]bove all things, whether he had control over himself. For an actor who possesses no self-possession, who cannot appear before a stranger in his most favorable light, has, generally speaking, little talent. His whole profession requires continual self-denial . . .[9]

Goethe's idea of self-control corresponds to the concept of moderation in Platonic philosophy. Self-control is not only an essential quality for actors but is arguably the foremost prerequisite for the development of character.

One of the central teachings of Buddhist philosophy bears directly on the question of character formation. Buddhism classifies the states of life that constitute human experience into ten worlds or realms. From the least to the most desirable they are: the world of hell, a condition submerged in suffering; the world of hunger, a state in which body and mind are engulfed in the raging flames of desire; the world of animality, in which one fears the strong and abuses the weak; the world of anger, characterized by the constant compulsion to surpass and dominate others; the world of humanity, a tranquil state marked by the ability to make reasoned judgments; the world of rapture, a state filled with joy; the world of learning, a condition of aspiration to enlightenment; the world of absorption, where one perceives unaided the true nature of phenomena; the world of Bodhisattva, a state of compassion in which one seeks to save all people from suffering; and finally the world of Buddhahood, a state of human completeness and perfect freedom.

Within each of these ten states or worlds is likewise to be found the full spectrum of the ten worlds. In other words, the state of hell contains within it every state from hell to Buddhahood. In the Buddhist view, life is never static, but is in constant flux, effecting a dynamic, moment-by-moment transformation among the states. The most critical point, then, is which of these ten states, as they exist in the vibrant flow of life, forms the basis for our own lives? Buddhism offers a way of life centered on the highest states, those of Bodhisattva and Buddhahood, as an ideal of human existence. Emotions—joy and sorrow, pleasure and anger—are of course the threads from which life's fabric is woven, and we continue to experience the full span of the ten worlds. These experiences, however, can be shaped and directed by the pure and indestructible states of Bodhisattva and Buddhahood. Nichiren, whose Buddhist teaching is the base of our organization, did more than merely preach this doctrine; he lived it, providing a remarkable model for the future. When, for example, he was about to be executed by the iniquitous authorities of the time, he reproached his lamenting disciples, saying, "What greater joy could there be?"[10] After overcoming the greatest trial of his life, he even had saké brought for the soldiers who had been escorting him to his execution.

Because of these qualities, I am confident that Buddhism can deeply affect the formation of character, which is the key to the restoration of human wholeness. As a practitioner of Buddhism, it is my hope that, together with our distinguished friends gathered here today, we will set off on a courageous journey in search of those new principles of integration that will determine the fate of humankind in the coming century. I would like to close by quoting a passage from a poem by Walt Whitman, whose poetry I have read and loved since my youth.

> I see male and female everywhere,
> I see the serene brotherhood of philosophs,
> I see the constructiveness of my race,
> I see the results of the perseverance and industry of my race,
> I see ranks, colors, barbarisms, civilizations, I go among them, I
> mix indiscriminately,
> And I salute all the inhabitants of the earth.[11]

NOTES

1. Procrustes was a mythical Greek robber who stretched or lopped off the limbs of his "guests" in order to make them fit the size of his bed.

2. From an interview with Dr. Joel Elkes, *Seikyo Shimbun,* July 8, 1992, 3.

3. D. H. Lawrence, *Apocalypse* (New York: Penguin Books, 1976), 125.

4. Eduard Heimann, *Soziale Theorie der Wirtschaftssysteme* (Hamburg: J.C.B. Mohr Tübingen, 1963), 36.

5. Chingiz Aitmatov and Daisaku Ikeda, *Ooinaru tamashii no uta* (Tokyo: Yomiuri Shimbunsha, 1991), 81.

6. Friedrich A. Hayek, *The Road to Serfdom* (Chicago: The University of Chicago Press, 1972), 17.

7. Scott Buchannan, ed., *The Portable Plato,* trans. Benjamin Jowett, ed. Scott Buchanan (New York: Viking Press, 1973), 238.

8. Walter Lippmann, *Public Opinion* (New York: Macmillan, 1938), 402ff.

9. Johann Peter Eckermann, *Conversations with Goethe,* trans. John Oxenford, ed. J. K. Moorhead (London: Everyman's Library, 1972), 100.

10. Philip B. Yampolsky, ed., *Selected Writings of Nichiren,* trans. Burton Watson et al., (New York: Columbia University Press, 1990), 326.

11. Walt Whitman, *Leaves of Grass* (New York: Random House, 1950), 116.

An Infinite Horizon

*A speech delivered at Shenzhen University, Guangdong,
January 31, 1994*

In 1993, when Dr. Cai Delin, president of Shenzhen University, visited Japan, he conferred upon me the title of professor emeritus. I regard this as the highest honor, and would like to thank him again. On the occasion of his visit, we reached an agreement regarding educational exchange between Shenzhen and Soka universities. Let us celebrate together this auspicious beginning to what I know will be a long and fruitful friendship.

My first trip to Shenzhen was in May 1974. Returning now, two decades later, I am astonished at the splendid development and healthy variety of activity that I see. The forest of multistory buildings, the fine, modern roads, the people from all over Asia who mingle here in this bustling city, are all evidence of Shenzhen's rapid advancement. As one who has always championed China's prosperity and long been involved in efforts for good relations between our countries, I am overjoyed.

Building a New World System

Still shaken by the shock waves of change that have raced through Eastern Europe and the former Soviet Union, the world faces a new, post–Cold War era. It began with hope as, only a few years ago, resurgent democratization seemed to sweep around the world. That tide has receded, pushed aside by a seemingly endless chain of ethnic and religious conflicts. People are confused about how to resolve these crises and are uncertain how to respond. It is not yet clear how to build a system that will replace the moribund Cold War framework and protect world peace.

For decades, the global order was maintained by the United States and the Soviet Union. For better or for worse, the two super-powers could use pressure tactics to prevent the escalation of hostilities between rival nations. What instruments do we have now to rein in the regional conflicts that continually threaten world peace? One possible force for stability is the United Nations, though it is often too weak to be effective. Furthermore, as the peacekeeping operation in Somalia has shown, the danger of getting hopelessly caught in civil war or domestic strife is always present.

At the end of last year I met with United Nations Secretary-General Boutros Boutros-Ghali in Tokyo. We spoke about the future of his organization and many other related subjects. I greatly admire the devoted efforts and hard work of the many people, both within and outside the United Nations, who are trying to find solutions to the intractable problems on the international front. Those of us, including SGI, who are working toward similar goals on the private level are always ready to support and encourage their efforts in any way we possibly can.

Yet, we must not forget the larger issue, the source of this black cloud hanging over the last years of our century. Many factors feed into this end-of-the-century malaise, but one of the most obvious is the desolate psychological state, particularly among people in the advanced industrial countries of the West. Far too many of them, lacking any plan or compass to guide their future, are wandering aimlessly. Our societies also are being eaten away by racism, drugs, violence, the decline of education, and the breakdown of the family unit. However one wishes to explain it, there is too much tolerance of unchecked passions and undisciplined, base behavior.

Max Weber (1864-1920) was one who saw this kind of development coming. At the conclusion of his study of the contributions from religion to European capitalism, he envisioned the appearance in mature capitalist societies of arrogant "specialists without spirit" and "sensualists without heart."[1] It was speculation, not prediction, but with hindsight we can see that there were grounds for his fears.

People Without Spirit

Several years ago, Francis Fukuyama's book, *The End of History and the Last Man,* was pubished amid extensive media coverage just at the time the Cold War was ending. Fukuyama borrowed from Nietzsche to describe the "last man" who would appear at the "end of history." His men with "desire" and "reason" are eerily like Weber's "sensualists without heart" and "specialists without spirit."

> Liberal democracy produced "men without chests," composed of desire and reason but lacking *thymos* (spiritedness), clever at finding new ways to satisfy a host of petty wants through the calculation of long-term self-interest.[2]

Such are the symptoms of no less than a crisis of civilization, and the core of the crisis is the potential loss of the very criteria by which humanity is defined. We must ask, once again, what we can do to restore our "spirit." For one thing, we should stop and listen carefully to our hidden streams of culture, what Arnold Toynbee called "the deeper, slower movements that, in the end, make history."[3] If Toynbee were thinking of Asia, he might have been describing a distinct current of humanism that has flowed continuously through Asian cultures, particularly the three thousand years of Chinese history. This tradition of humanism has fueled China's remarkable economic growth in recent years.

Twenty years ago, Joseph Needham, the preeminent authority in Chinese studies, delivered an address at Hong Kong University. He remarked that in this age of the dusk of the gods it is appropriate to seek "a conception of morality, an ethical model, which was never supported by supernatural sanctions."[4] In that search, he proclaimed,

"It is just here that Chinese culture may have, it seems to me, an invaluable gift to make to the world."[5]

The Christian God is a good example of what Needham meant by "the supernatural." In the West, systems of ethical thought are premised on acknowledgment and affirmation of supernatural agencies, which means, above all, on a covenant with God. Judeo-Christian ethics are the consequence of a pact between God and his mortal "children." Only secondarily are ethics considered in terms of a covenant among people. The famous thirteen virtues of Benjamin Franklin (temperance, silence, order, resolution, frugality, industry, sincerity, justice, moderation, cleanliness, tranquillity, chastity, and humility)[6], for example, are the unmistakable fruit of Greek and Christian thought. But they also contain a universality that transcends their cultural or philosophic derivation. They are, in fact, somewhat similar to traditional Chinese virtues, in particular, the Confucian virtues of humaneness, righteousness, propriety, wisdom, and fidelity. The similarity helps to explain the enthusiasm with which Benjamin Franklin was lionized by Japanese of the Meiji period (1868–1912), beginning with the enlightenment thinker and educator Yukichi Fukuzawa (1834–1901).

There are differences, however, between the Confucian virtues and Franklin's, one of which hinges on the Western concept of a covenant with God. The thirteen virtues are a classical expression of the ethos of the period when capitalism took hold in the United States. They were supported by the a confidence that suppression of personal desires and accumulation of wealth were signs of divine favor and were a testament to God's glory.

That belief produced many highly disciplined, charitable people such as Franklin, who were attractive models for behavior. However, as one hundred, then two hundred years passed and faith in God became less assured, the virtues that were part and parcel of that faith lost potency as a guide to living. As a result, it can be argued that contemporary industrial society closely resembles Fukuyama's portrayal. This is precisely why our age needs ethical models grounded in human nature that do not require the recognition or affirmation of God, or any supernatural being.

Self and the Individual

The motto of Shenzhen University is "Self-Reliance, Self-Discipline, Self-Improvement." Standing on one's own feet, disciplining oneself, and strengthening oneself—these ideals are aimed at creating the tenacious, towering individuals who will shoulder the responsibilities for China's future. The concept of "self" in the motto is very different from the notion of "the individual" in Western culture. An individual in the West has the connotation of separability, being the smallest indivisible unit of human society, and as such, an individual is ultimately an isolated being. The "self" of Chinese philosophy is not bound so strictly and implies an inherent linkage with other beings.

Professor William Theodore de Bary of Columbia University investigated the use of Chinese words beginning with the prefix *zi-* (self) in the history of thought of the Song and Ming dynasties. Some examples of Chinese words beginning with this prefix are *ziran* (natural), *zide* (self-possessed) and *ziren* (taking it upon oneself). De Bary says: "One could compile a virtual lexicon of terms with the prefix *Zi- (tzu-)* which recur frequently [in the discussions of the Neo-Confucians]."[7] It seems that an entire dictionary reflecting a complex and varied ethical tapestry can be created from the term "self." Into it would be woven the strength and importance of the traditional Chinese view of humankind.

It is noteworthy that the character for "person" (*ren*) shows two people leaning on each other. This, I think, is a vital key to Chinese thought. The character for "humaneness" (also pronounced *ren*) is composed of the characters for "person" and the number two, meaning two people facing one another, two people communicating with each other, two people who love each other. The implication is that there is no such thing as an isolated individual.

Individuals are linked together in a single living entity. Their bonds are not limited to the human world, but extend to the natural world and to the cosmos, making all existence one organic whole. This traditional Chinese view of humanity and nature was strongly influenced by the Neo-Confucianism of Zhu Xi in the Song dynasty. In Neo-Confucian thought, the relationships and interdependence of things—including human beings—are more important than their existence as discrete entities. This view is profoundly linked to the Buddhist teaching of *pratitya-samutpada,* or the law of dependent origination (*engi* in Japanese).

It is an organic view of humanity that recognizes no phenomenon in the universe as unrelated to humankind. Everything is included in the question, "How should we live?" In this "human-scaled" way of thinking, all things are measured in terms of people. Science exists to serve people; government, economics, and ideology serve people. The meaning of good and evil, abundance and deficiency, in fact, all phenomena are measured on this scale of service to humankind. This kind of humanism is present in all Eastern schools of thought, but appears in its classic form in Chinese philosophy.

Sun Yat-sen's Humanism

It is interesting to read the work of Sun Yat-sen, who demonstrated a deep understanding of Eastern humanism. His unique definition of freedom is set forth in *San Min Chu I* (The Three Principles of the People), in which he asks how the word "freedom" is to be used. He suggests that if we use it to refer to the individual, society will resemble the separate grains in a handful of sand. This statement might seem to be the rationalization of an authoritarian nationalist, but it was part of a larger argument relating to the rights of the people. In a larger context, it becomes the testimony of a person dedicated to freedom, rather than the justification of a would-be dictator. For Sun Yat-sen, freedom is not just a printed word or a concept but a living reality that vibrates in the people's immediate experience and sentiments. An abstract notion of freedom that is applied universally is a phantom; it can never be realized by compulsion. True freedom must be sought in, and built from, the reality in which we live.

Sun Yat-sen maintained that the goals of any common struggle must cut deeply under the skin. Otherwise, people will not be engaged. The expression "human reality" is just another way of saying "the people's actual experience and sentiments in life." Alienated from the experiences of life, there is no such thing as freedom for the people, for the two become reversed. People do not exist for the sake of freedom.

Chinese pragmatism is characterized by the ability to embrace apparent logical contradictions and irrationalities in the complex totality of a culture. It rejects the temptation to resolve conflicting elements of society by forcing a direct confrontation between them. This is a flexible and generous type of humanism that is basically opposed to forcing a choice between two alternatives. So the Chinese philosophical tradition, as seen in the concept of the Great Harmony (Da Tong), has favored a holistic approach in which potential conflict is avoided by unifying the alternatives. Sun Yat-sen's concept of freedom, which he discovered not in books but in the constant change of real life as it moves from moment to moment, is a product of this holistic approach.

It is easy to make a connection between this approach and China's recent policy of combining socialism and the free market. Since it went into effect in the autumn of 1992, that policy has been widely discussed both inside and outside China. From one perspective it may seem that grafting the free market, the cradle of capitalism, to socialism (which is defined by a planned economy) would be as difficult as an attempt to graft bamboo to an oak. But if we distance ourselves from government and economics and think in terms of holistic, unifying humanism, suddenly the "socialist market economy" takes on a very different hue. Consider what Deng Xiaoping said about the introduction of free-market institutions or even a stock exchange:

> Let us approve it and try it with determination. If it works, if after one or two years it works, let us liberalize it. If it doesn't work, let us revise it before we abandon it. As for abandoning it, we can abandon it quickly, abandon it slowly, or leave certain traces of it. What do we have to be afraid of? If we firmly uphold this attitude, nothing bad should occur. We will not make a major error.[8]

This is truly a flexible and generous attitude. I met with Deng on two occasions, on my second and third visits to China, and on both occasions he shared with me his vision of China's development and prosperity. His policy of using a human scale to judge what is appropriate and inappropriate in the "socialist market economy" is a superbly humanist idea. It ensures the development of an economy for the people; an economy that does not unsettle their lives.

A Socialist Market Economy

The gradual method that has been adopted in introducing the market economy is an example of the cautious approach. Instead of launching changes everywhere at the same time, special zones such as Shenzhen have been established as experimental areas. By limiting the implementation of the market economy to certain regions, results can be monitored, adjustments made, and policies improved based on performance.

I believe that the gradual approach to developing the "socialist market economy," despite its incongruent tone, represented a critical choice for China, particularly in view of the many difficulties the nation faces as it moves forward. It is a choice that minimizes the negative effects of historical retrenchment and aims for social stability and growth. Considering the vast population and area of China, this historical experiment will have a tremendous effect on people everywhere in the twenty-first century. The world is watching China's efforts expectantly, and as an old friend, I also am praying for your success.

In the end, everything starts with the people and returns to the people. In economics, as in all other things, we must exercise the kind of "human-scale" control expressed in the Confucian dictum that virtue is the root and wealth is the result. Failing this, we will only encourage the tendency to worship wealth, a sickness that is already too widespread. When Joseph Needham speaks of "a conception of morality" and "an ethical model," he is proposing the antithesis of that tendency. And when Toynbee wrote, "Perhaps it is China's destiny now to give political unity and peace not just to half but to all the world,"[9] he was anticipating the spread of the humanistic moral force that China has accumulated over its long history. I believe that here in Shenzhen, as you look toward the next century with a spirit of self-reliance, self-discipline, and self-improvement, the humanism recognized by both Needham and Toynbee lies on the horizon.

Let me close by borrowing the words of the great poet Bo Juyi:

> Give your full energies
> To communication with good friends
> Always take care
> To make honest people your companions.

NOTES

1. Max Weber, *The Protestant Ethic and the Spirit of Capitalism,* trans. Talcott Parsons (London: Unwin University Books, 1970), 182.

2. Francis Fukuyama, *The End of History and the Last Man* (New York: Penguin Books, 1992), 300.

3. Arnold J. Toynbee, *Civilization on Trial and the World and the West* (Cleveland and New York: The World Publishing Company, 1968), 188.

4. Joseph Needham, *Moulds of Understanding: A Pattern of Natural Philosophy,* ed. Gary Werskey (London: George Allen & Unwin Ltd., 1976), 302.

5 Ibid., 301.

6. Benjamin Franklin, *The Autobiography and Selections from His Other Writings,* ed. Herbert W. Schneider (New York: The Liberal Arts Press, 1952), 81-83.

7. Wm. Theodore de Bary, *The Liberal Tradition in China* (New York: Columbia University Press, 1983), 44.

8. Deng Xiaoping, *Deng Xiaoping Wenxuan* (Selections from Deng Xiaoping's Writings), (Beijing: People's Publishing House, 1993), 3:373.

9. Arnold J. Toynbee and Daisaku Ikeda, *The Toynbee-Ikeda Dialogue: Man Himself Must Choose* (Tokyo: Kodansha International Ltd., 1976), 233.

A Garden of Imagination

A speech delivered at the Brazilian Academy of Letters,
Rio de Janeiro, February 12, 1993

Allow me to extend greetings to President Austregésilo de Athayde, the members of the Brazilian Academy of Letters, and all the honored guests.

The Brazilian Academy of Letters has bestowed on me not only the great honor of awarding me a seat as a nonresident member of the Academy, but also the Machado de Assis Medal. The seat was named after the remarkable rhetorician Francisco de Mont'Alverne from Rio de Janeiro. Its former occupants include the English philosopher Herbert Spencer, the French sociologist Jean Finot, the French writer Ernest Martinenche, the Spanish literary historian Ramón Menéndez Pidal, and the American translator William Grossman, who is known for his translations of the writings of the Academy's founder and first president, Machado de Assis. It is humbling to be designated the successor to such eminent individuals, the first Asian to have that privilege.

Hope Out of Chaos

According to Machado de Assis, who is also known as the father of contemporary Brazilian literature, the Brazilian Academy of Letters, founded in the late nineteenth century, was modeled after the Institut de France. The Academy was intended to be an assembly of youthful Brazilians dedicated to promoting new ideas and new ways of thinking. When I was invited in 1989 to speak at the Institut de France, I closed that lecture with a poem I had written:

> And here is Art,
> Inviting the soul by reaching her hand out
> Toward a soothing and serene wood,
> Toward a garden where imagination blazes across the sky;
> Inviting it to the noble stage of wisdom
> And leading it toward the far-off horizon
> Of universal civilization.

Science and technology may be rapidly forging our world into a single entity, but we cannot look forward to a better tomorrow unless we are spiritually prepared. We must aspire toward what might be called a universal civilization.

Thinking optimistically, the collapse of ideology will lead to pluralism; in the pessimistic view, it will lead to chaos. Given the necessity of seeking unity and harmony within diversity, the Brazilian experiment will be extremely important in leading the way toward a universal civilization. Known for its ethnically diverse democracy, Brazil may become an invaluable example for the future, helping us to avoid the kind of conditions that gave rise to the recent Los Angeles riots in the United States, to neo-Nazism in Germany, and other divisive events.

The Brazilian character has been described by Sérgio Buarque de Holanda in his classic works. He writes:

> The virtues that visitors to Brazil all praise in chorus—the openness, kindness, hospitality, and generosity of spirit— must become traits that will never disappear.[1]

Japanese acquaintances of mine who have made this country their home agree with that description. Several years ago, I spoke with

Ryoichi Kodama, a first-generation Japanese immigrant who had lived here for eighty years. He cheerfully declared, "I love the whole of Brazilian nature. I really love Brazil, and if you ask me where I'd like to be born in my next life, I'd say Brazil."[2]

What lies at the heart of this character that has charmed so many people? After reading the masterpiece *Grande Sertão: Veredas* (*The Devil to Pay in the Backlands*) which was written by the twentieth-century Brazilian writer (and former member of this esteemed academy) João Guimarães Rosa, I believe that the Brazilian temperament has its spiritual foundation in a great universality.

Over the last several centuries, European civilization has disseminated a scientific and technological brand of universalism throughout the entire globe. With an unrelenting drive for efficiency and expansion, it has forcibly brought the world under its influence. Arnold Toynbee discusses this phenomenon in *The World and the West,* in which he says that each nation has found that it must define its future according to its reaction to European civilization. Since the 1920s, the great minds of Brazil have debated this theme, using modernism or regionalism as their frame of reference.

The universalism of modern science is not genuine universalism. In an abstract and self-defining world disconnected from values and meaning, a culture based on science and technology may be both pervasive and uniform, but it is no more than the skin of the fruit. It does not touch the sum total of human life. Rather than being universal, it is actually a very specific and particular element, and only one of many, in a culture.

The Closed Box and the Open Box

Dr. Fred Hoyle, an astronomer at Cambridge University, talks about universality using the metaphor of a "closed" versus an "open" box in his prefatory remarks to a dialogue between myself and his student, Sri Lankan-born astronomer Dr. N. Chandra Wickramasinghe. According to Dr. Hoyle, modern science is based on a geocentrically conceived universe, an idea that appeared around the year 500 A.D. He describes this idea as the "closed box," stating:

Nothing which happens here on Earth can have any conceivable relation to events in the Universe outside the Earth, except of course for the beneficial heating effect of the Sun.[3]

If the closed box is metaphorically a narrow, parochial mindset, it does not offer the best means to solve issues of any scope. It is a frame of mind that ultimately cuts out any outside influence; it is egocentric prejudice. The human propensity to think in this manner damages more than just the area of science. Its influence can have a negative effect on our entire worldview. The geocentrism embedded in much of modern science is echoed in the anthropocentrism and ethnocentrism that have penetrated modern civilization. Such perspectives are all products of the same closed-box model.

Another effect of this type of thinking is colonialism. Having provided a rationale for outsiders to exert control in Asia, Latin America, and Africa, colonialist assumptions continue to cast their spell. They are so deeply rooted that even scientists, no matter how well-intentioned, often do not fully recognize them. The ethnocentrism that shaped colonialist policies and grew stronger as a consequence of them went largely unremarked for a long time, partly because colonialism was, in fact, often motivated by an accepted, if misplaced, sense of duty or mission.

This mindset could be loosened by an "open-box" approach to life and the universe. Dr. Hoyle noted such broadness in the dialogue between Dr. Wickramasinghe and myself, commenting that perhaps our thinking reflected our both being Asians who share the cultural traditions of Buddhism.

The consequences of the closed-box model as it relates to ethnocentrism are dramatically illustrated in the book *Heart of Darkness* by the Polish-born English novelist Joseph Conrad. Employed as a crewman on a boat harvesting ivory, Conrad sailed up the Congo River and witnessed first-hand the exploitation of black Africans by white Europeans. His subsequent writing on this theme is unrivaled in its realism. One passage speaks of the conquest of the earth. Conrad writes that conquest, for the most part, brings ruin and despoliation to people of different complexions, and:

[The conquest of the earth] is not a pretty thing when you look into it too much. What redeems it is the idea only. An idea at the back of it; not a sentimental pretense but an idea; and an unselfish belief in the idea—something you can set up, and bow down before, and offer a sacrifice to. . .[4]

Here Conrad vividly portrays the impersonal universalism that is the inverse of the barbaric passion of colonialism. The "idea" is irrefutably a product of the closed box. It may seem compelling, but beside the open-box approach, it is revealed as obscene prejudice. It is sufficient to remember the terrifying devastation of human beings who came into contact with the followers of what Conrad labeled "idea."

The closed-box way of thinking has not only spawned colonialism, but has created a framework for modern civilization. Sensitivity to the suffering of others, as well as the ability to understand and accept different cultures and peoples, have been squeezed out of modern life. The balance between intellect and emotion, empathy with nature and the cosmos, and awe for great things seem to be missing for many of us. Yet those qualities resonate through Holanda's description of Brazil and Brazilians.

There is no doubt a dark side to Brazil, also. The poet Carlos Drummond de Andrade described his country with resignation: "So majestic, so endless, so absurd, / She wants to reject our terrible affection."[5] As he eloquently put it, the Brazilian spirit alternates between light and darkness in a dizzying fashion that defies simple description. Nonetheless I see in the Brazilian spirit, even if its contours are not yet clear, a route to a great universalism that can replace the superficial one of modern society.

Hope for the Future

Recently, Soka Gakkai International held an exhibition entitled "The Environment and Development" as part of the Earth Summit held in Brazil. During the exhibition's symposium, President Athayde spoke here in the new lecture hall of the Academy of Letters. In his speech, he stated:

The Brazilian people are a great people. They are the fount of our hope. If we are to meet the many challenges we will face in the new century, we must rely on the Brazilian people, the hope of our country.

The greatness of a people is reflected in their art and literature. In many of the developed countries art has lost vitality, leaving a "wasteland," in T.S. Eliot's words, or a "dry spring," in Paul Valéry's phrase. In contrast, the literature of Brazil, and indeed of all Latin America, demonstrates an acute awareness of the current world crisis of the spirit and radiates a fierce energy directed toward the formation of a new universal order.

Two very cosmopolitan Europeans, Michel de Montaigne and Stefan Zweig lived tumultuous lives at the beginning and the end, respectively, of the modern European age. It is intriguing that both were seekers of universal spiritual values and each had a burning interest in Brazil. Montaigne learned of this country from a servant who had spent more than ten years here. At that time the nation of Brazil did not exist; it was the customs of the native people that fascinated Montaigne. In contrast, Zweig experienced Brazil in the mid-twentieth century when it had become an advanced, ethnically diverse democracy. Pursued by the Nazis, Zweig chose this country as his place of refuge. The coincidental parallel between these two men in particular seems significant. In fact, while he was in Brazil, and with death near, Zweig avidly read the works of Montaigne.

I have enjoyed reading Montaigne's *Essays* since my youth. In this massive work, which is a treasury of wisdom, the section describing Brazilian customs stands out:

> I do not believe, from what I have been told about this people, that there is anything barbarous or savage about them, except that we all call barbarous anything that is contrary to our own habits. Indeed we seem to have no other criterion of truth and reason than the type and kind of opinions and customs current in the land where we live.[6]

These quiet and reasoned thoughts on the customs of an indigenous American society were actually quite shocking and courageous, given the conventional wisdom of the time. Montaigne's unclouded vision predates by some four centuries the paradigm of cultural relativism—sometimes called the "discovery of the primitive"—in twentieth-century anthropology.

Montaigne reminds us that the ability to perceive things from another's point of view is required of a true cosmopolitan. It is a kind of open-box thinking. A one-sided viewpoint that reduces everything to a single standard cannot ever be called "universalist."

Driven from his homeland, Stefan Zweig lamented, "For all that I had been training my heart for almost half a century to beat as that of a *citoyen du monde,* it was useless."[7] Sunk in disappointment and pain, Zweig was warmly embraced and comforted by the great land of Brazil. In this sense, there are few passages that speak more articulately of the accepting Brazilian nature than his will, which was appended to his book *The World of Yesterday:*

> My love for the country increased from day to day, and nowhere else would I have preferred to build up a new existence, the world of my own language having disappeared for me, and my spiritual home, Europe, having destroyed itself.[8]

Two world wars and the Nazi genocide amounted to our civilization's attempt at suicide. It took little reflection to realize how savage the denizens of sophisticated, highly advanced societies could be. Having seen those horrors, Zweig must have felt an immediate identification with Montaigne. Though long dead, here was a kindred spirit proclaiming that in comparison with ourselves, we can never call anyone else barbarian, no matter how "primitive," for "we surpass them in every kind of barbarity."[9]

The Universal Within the Particular

I learned a great deal about Brazil from the book *The Modern Culture of Latin America: Society and the Artist,* by Jean Franco, the English pioneer of Latin American studies. In this book, Franco suggests that tension is a distinctive feature of twentieth-century Brazilian culture:

> A prominent feature of Brazilian cultural life in the last forty years is the tension between the need for roots and the urge for modernity, between those who want to stress local or regional characteristics and those who want Brazil to be in the forefront of world culture.[10]

This succinct evaluation captures part of the essence of Brazilian culture. The rich fruits of Brazil's great universalism can only be harvested where the tension of particulars is present. Torn apart by ideologies of race and class, the people of our century have paid a great price to learn the vital lesson that universalism divorced from particulars can too easily become the dangerous self-centeredness Conrad warned about in his discussion of "idea."

True universality must be sought within the particular. The infusion of the one into the other creates a state of constant tension between the two. Sustaining that tension is the task of art, whose value lies in the imaginative power to evoke the universal lying within the particular. Mahayana Buddhism orients us to the same kind of creative tension. Nichiren Daishonin, whose teachings guide the members of Soka Gakkai International, defines the Mahayana spirit as follows: "The eighty-four thousand teachings that Shakyamuni preached during his lifetime are the diary of one's own being." And, "The example of one person represents the impartial truth inherent in all human beings."[11] In other words, universal teachings and concepts do not possess any significance of their own. They unfold concretely within the life of each person.

The fastest way to discover the fine qualities of a people is to search the minds of their great writers. João Guimarães Rosa's *The Devil to Pay in the Backlands* tells us much about Brazil as it examines issues of roots and modernity. There is a compelling power in the bold, abrupt, and cosmic pronouncement of the young *jagunço* (ruffian) Riobaldo during his fierce struggle in the wilds of northeastern Brazil: "I would like to found a city based on religion."[12] Could anyone speak of religion with such invigorating innocence in our world today?

Contemporary religion has a myriad of forms and qualities. It may be so completely laicized that it survives informally in name, or in external form only, or it may be reduced to an intensely internal and personal matter. Sometimes it is a mixture of occult practices and superstition. Religions experience periods of growth and contraction, or suddenly explode with energy, triggering bloody conflict. These are all negative images; it seems that religion is rarely talked about in a positive, hopeful way today. In the person of Riobaldo, however, we find a character who speaks of religion with expectation and warmth. Although he is rough and wild in appearance, his heart beats with fine sensitivity in response to questions about the covenant between God and the devil, and the nature of love, trust, freedom, and courage.

The attempt to master the *sertão,* the backlands, is not simply a battle for hegemony. It is a struggle to establish justice; a blow struck by an awakening sense of mission. Developing, it becomes an internal battle as well. Thus, Ribaldo says:

We have got to wake up the *sertão!* But the only way to wake the *sertão* is to do so from within.[13]

The *sertão*—it is inside of one.[14]

The meaning of the *sertão* expands from specific "backlands" to become a universal symbol of our internal "backlands." Furthermore, "a city based on religion" is a highly abstract symbol of that which has been internalized and has shed its profane nature to become the "manifestation of the sacred." Religion in this sense embraces and unifies humankind, nature, and the universe. It is the source of energy for the revitalization of the cosmos. Because he understands religion in that way, Riobaldo's words contain a reality and substance that could be called "great universalism."

Healing the Madness

Rosa's reality is grounded in a tenacious attachment to the particular. He found his material in the primitive world of a *jagunço,* whose *sertao* he describes in detail worthy of a naturalist and geologist, and whose popular lore is liberally woven into the text. His choices for setting and background have the same effect as the background of the "Mona Lisa"—those rocky spires rising in perfect perspective, so poignantly setting off the Giaconda's smile.

Rosa sees the way to an answer for a troubled world in religion, but not in dogma. It is prayer that will save us. He writes:

> What I firmly believe, declare, and set forth, is this: the whole world is crazy. You, sir, I, we, everybody. That's the main reason we need religion: to become unmaddened, regain our sanity. Praying is what cures madness. Usually. It is the salvation of the soul.[15]

Far from healing, dogma can only fan the flames of madness and fanaticism. In the type of religious world Rosa anticipates, religion cultivates and elevates human spirituality while providing the foundation for the construction of a new cosmos. It represents the ideal of the great universalism that must become the backbone of world civilization in the twenty-first century. I have pledged my own energies to building the foundation for that universal spirit.

In closing, let us envision Brazil's infinite future with some lines of verse from *"Ode ao Dous de Julho"* by the great nineteenth Brazilian poet Castro Alves.

> Yes!
> Through our fingers,
> The sands of time have slipped
> Until at last,
> A century is about to expire,

In a certain country
The names of great persons
Will be discovered in plenty—
More than our hands can hold.

O!
You heroes!
Like the majestic cedars
Which even after long centuries
Tower strong and undefeated
You are the great trees of history
And
In the shade of your glory
Brazil rests.[16]

NOTES

1. Sérgio Buarque de Holanda, *Burajirujin towa nanika* (Tokyo: Shin Sekaisha, 1976), 166.

2. Daisaku Ikeda and Ryoichi Kodama, *Taiyo to Daichi—Kaitaku no Kyoku* (The Sun and the Earth—A Song of Pioneers) (Tokyo: Daisan Bunmei-sha publishing Co., Ltd., 1991), 185.

3. Chandra Wickramasinghe and Daisaku Ikeda, *Uchu to Ningen no Roman wo Kataru* (Romance on Man and the Universe), (Tokyo: The Mainichi Shimbun, 1992), 2–3.

4. Joseph Conrad, *Heart of Darkness* (New York: Penguin Books, 1973), 32.

5. Carlos Drummond de Andrade, "Hino Nacioal," *Reunião-10 Livros de Poesia* (Rio de Janeiro: José Olympio Editora, 1978), 37.

6. Michel de Montaigne, *Essays,* trans. J. M. Cohen (New York: Penguin Books, 1958), 108.

7. Stefan Zweig, *The World of Yesterday* (Lincoln: University of Nebraska Press, 1964), 412.

8. Ibid., 437.

9. Montaigne, 114.

10. Jean Franco, *The Modern Culture of Latin America: Society and the Artist* (New York: Frederick A. Praeger, 1967), 267.

11. Nichiko Hori, ed., *Nichiren Daishonin Gosho Zenshu,* (Tokyo: Soka Gakkai, 1952), 563–564.

12. João Guimarães Rosa, *The Devil to Pay in the Backlands,* trans. James L. Taylor and Harriet de Onas (New York: Alfred A. Knopf, 1963), 257.

13. Ibid., 232.

14. Ibid., 257.

15. Ibid., 10.

16. Castro Alves, "Ode Ao Dous de Julho," in *Castro Alves por Eugênio Gomes.* (Rio de Janeiro: Livraria AGIR Editôra, 1963), 42–44.

Globalism and Nationalism

A speech delivered at the University of Buenos Aires,
March 1, 1990[1]

This is a memorable day for me. First, I have the honor to speak at one of the most prestigious institutions of higher learning in Latin America, and I want to thank Rector Shuberoff, the faculty, and the student body of the Universidád de Buenos Aires for giving me this opportunity. Second, I extend to the university my sincere gratitude for the honorary degree conferred on me. It presents me with a high standard that I will try to live up to.

A Borderless World

Today we are living in what, in many respects, can be called a "borderless world." National boundaries have become less significant in an increasing range of endeavors, including finance, trade, and technology. Toward the end of 1989, the Berlin wall, symbol of the Cold War, collapsed. Having visited Berlin, I was all the more affected as we watched the tide of history turn. The events commanded us to acknowledge that global interdependence, both political and economic, is growing all the time; it is no longer possible for any state or regime to hold onto a policy of isolationism.

A great transition is in the making. The gears of history, long confined to a tragic repetition of confrontation and division, have finally begun creaking out of the old pattern toward a new order of coexistence and harmony. Their smooth rotation forward is slowed, however, by the stubborn force of inertia, namely our assumptions about how we relate to the world. Thus, the greatest challenge we face on the eve of the twenty-first century is to shift gears and find a way to harmonize and fuse nationalism and globalism. We will have to do no less than redefine and reorient nationalism in the context of a united world, the global village. The upheaval of the post-Yalta years has already had a forceful impact. It can be seen in ethnic strife in the Soviet Union and Eastern Europe, in the agonies of German unification, and in the movement toward integration of the European Community. Failure to manage these issues well could lead to uncontrollable confusion, and the sun of world unity just visible over the far horizon would be shut out by heavy clouds.

Earlier in 1990, I met Ambassador De la Guardia in Tokyo. At that time he offered a perceptive description of Argentina's national character. It is hard to make a quick generalization, he said, but perhaps his country might be called a "land of harmonious fusion." I was impressed at this unexpected, insightful characterization. Geographically, Argentina is exceedingly diverse; one can find widely different landscapes without ever leaving the country. Its people, also, come from many different ethnic groups. The single nation that they have worked for, a fusion of many people, represents the type of transformation that is necessary if we are to make optimum use of the potential of the future.

The process of fusion may seem chaotic, but there is order in it. It is like a whirlpool that generates a new cosmos out of a jumble. Within the vortex, where the chaos seems most extreme, the movement of human life is dynamic and at its most creative. This might be the image of Argentina today, a multiracial land where the process of fusion is underway. The energy produced here is enormous, seeming on the verge of boiling over, but instead of dissipating, it builds. What is happening in Argentina looks exactly like the "generative chaos" used by French sociologist Edgar Morin to describe Europe. That is why I see Argentina as a forerunner of the new globalism.

A New Image of Humanity

A borderless world requires a new image of humanity that suits the times. In that perspective, the kind of individualism that has taken root here in Argentina is striking. Argentina has proudly maintained a spirit of freedom and autonomy as one of the first countries in Latin America to establish independence. Its people have achieved a multiracial unity and created a flourishing cosmopolitan ethos. Argentina provides a valuable example of an amicable marriage between the autonomous individual and the citizen of the world.

The Argentine poet and writer Jorge Luis Borges, who wrote of his vision of a labyrinth that exists outside time and space, stated that, "The only immortal being is humanity itself." He himself made the wondrous discovery that one person embraces all others; that all human beings can be realized in one individual. Phrased differently, by delving vertically into the inner layers of one's own mind, one comes upon universality. According to Borges, the Argentine people place more emphasis on being human beings than on being citizens. Thus, universality is attained by breaking through the "horizontal" framework of the nation-state. At the point where the "vertical" and "horizontal" dimensions meet is the image of the cosmopolitan individual, equipped with both personal autonomy and a global outlook.

One of Argentina's literary masterpieces is *Martin Fierro,* which depicts gauchos struggling for survival in the vast reaches of the pampas. Toward the end of this captivating work, the hero Martin Fierro says poetically:

> Happiness and unhappiness of all my brothers
> are my own happiness and unhappiness.
> In their proud minds
> will they bear my way of life.
> Forever will my paisanos
> remember me always.[2]

The usual image of the gaucho is a defiant and independent loner, verging sometimes on the outlaw. The very isolation of the gaucho makes the fond reference in the poem to other *paisanos* (peasants) all the more poignant. I am committed to the hope of a new age when people think of humankind in the same way as Martin Fierro does of his *paisanos.*

Among the truly difficult challenges of our era is the issue of human rights, which seems to grow more complex, more controversial, and more important by the day. A cosmopolitan people can make an invaluable contribution as we set out to meet that challenge. Ours is the era of "third-generation human rights." First- and second-generation human rights refer to the basic rights to freedom and to life, respectively. At present, it is the state that protects these rights, and to which appeals are directed. Third-generation human rights, however, embrace aspects of development, environment, and peace and cannot be attained without a coordinated, global effort unhindered by national boundaries.

Consider the right to a healthy environment. Measures to secure and safeguard a healthy environment may come to nothing if they are confined within state borders and pursued in the interests of one nation alone. A clean atmosphere and unpolluted water can be guaranteed only if we work with a global perspective that takes into account the interests of humankind as a whole.

The borderless world will offer unparalleled opportunities for the cosmopolitan. To achieve it, we must abandon exclusionist practices and concepts. At the personal level, each individual must understand in all practicality that one's own fate and the survival of the human race are one and the same. The issue of human rights, I believe, is part of a new and universalistic system of values. The national character of the people of Argentina, and the vigor and creativity of its youth, promise to give this country a leading role in the human rights movement.

NOTES

1. This speech was delivered by Mr. Hiromasa Ikeda on behalf of Daisaku Ikeda, his father.—Eds.

2. José Hernández, *Martin Fierro* (Buenos Aires: Instituto Salesiano de Artes Gráficas, 1972), 299.

The Age of Soft Power

A speech delivered at Harvard University, Cambridge,
September 26, 1991

It is an honor to be here today, but I feel especially privileged to have been invited to speak at this time, when Harvard University is commemorating three hundred and fifty five years of an illustrious history. I want to thank Professor John D. Montgomery of the Kennedy School for making this occasion possible, and professors Joseph Nye and Ashton Carter for their comments, among all the many people who have so kindly welcomed me here.

The recent political changes in the Soviet Union have shaken the world, calling attention to a momentous and unstoppable trend. It has been hailed as the rise of "soft power." In the past, the driving force of history all too often depended on the "hard power" of military might, political authority, and wealth. In recent years, however, the relative importance of hard power has diminished, slowly giving way to knowledge and information, culture, ideas, and systems—the weapons of soft power.

Although the conduct of the 1991 Gulf War might appear to be a classic example of the application of "hard" military power, the guns and tactics of the coalition forces first needed the "soft" power of United Nations support and positive world opinion to allow their use in the first place. I believe we have a historical obligation to encourage the steady reduction of the use of hard power, while ensuring the permanent substitution of soft power in its place.

I propose that self-motivation is what will open the way to the era of soft power. While systems depending on hard power have succeeded by using established tools of coercion to move people toward certain goals, the success of soft power is based on volition. It is an internally generated energy of will created through consensus and understanding among people. The processes of soft power unleash the inner energies of the individual. Rooted in the spirituality and religious nature of human beings, this kind of energy has traditionally been considered in philosophical themes. But without the support of a philosophical foundation to strengthen and mobilize the spiritual resources of the individual, the use of soft power would become nothing more than "fascism with a smile." In such a society information and knowledge would be abundant, but subject to manipulation by those in power. A citizenry without wisdom would fall easy prey to authority with self-serving goals. For these reasons, the burden of sustaining and accelerating the trend toward soft power lies with philosophy.

Religion and Individual Conscience

Let me offer an example to illustrate what I mean by self-motivation. In his *Les provinciales* (Provincial Letters), Blaise Pascal attacks the elaborate system of "precedents for the conscience" that were established by the Jesuits to facilitate missionary work. The nature of his attack sheds light on the fundamental difference between internally generated motivation and that which is imposed from without. The Jesuits had developed a highly elaborate system for the propagation of their faith. When expedience demanded, they went so far as to permit Christians to worship non-Christian deities. As a Jansenist, Pascal emphasized the importance of the individual conscience. He denounced the use of Church authority to establish and impose predetermined standards and precepts for the conscience. Pascal describes the practice:

This plan they followed in the Indies and in China, where they permitted Christians to practice idolatry itself, with the aid of the following ingenious contrivance: they made their converts conceal under their clothes an image of Jesus Christ, to which they taught themselves to transfer mentally those adorations which they rendered ostensibly to the idol [of Shakyamuni or Confucius].[1]

Pascal does not condemn the practice itself; he acknowledges that there might be times when it is necessary. The decision to deceive, however, can only be reached through a process of contemplation, self-questioning, and soul-searching, which add up to the workings of the individual conscience. If a preestablished standard or precedent for such a decision is provided from without, this painful process of self-examination is avoided. Instead of developing, the conscience atrophies. For Pascal, what the Jesuits called "precedents for the conscience" were nothing more than a servile surrender to the desire for easy answers. For him, they represented the suicide of the conscience, one's inner moral guidance. Pascal's criticism reaches beyond its particular historical context to address the universal question of the nature of human conscience.

Nineteenth-century America, while perhaps not evincing the level of purity that would have satisfied Pascal, provides one of history's rare cases when an emphasis on the inner workings of the soul set the tenor for an entire society. Visiting the United States a half-century after its founding, Alexis de Tocqueville was impressed above all by the simplicity of American religious practices and, at the same time, by their sincerity and depth of feeling. With analytical acuity, Tocqueville conveyed his impressions in *Democracy in America,* which contains the following passage:

It became my object . . . to inquire how it happened that the real authority of religion was increased by the state of things which diminished its apparent force . . .[2]

The Catholic church in France had visual and artistic impact, characterized by elaborate formality and complex ritual. Often, the effect was to fetter and restrain the spirit. Tocqueville had, therefore, assumed that any reduction in the church's "apparent force"—its formalities and its rituals—would free people from its external control, resulting in weaker faith. In America he found that the opposite was true. To quote him again:

> I have seen no country in which Christianity is clothed in fewer forms, figures, and observances than in the United States; or where it presents more distinct, more simple, or more commonly acceptable notions to the mind.[3]

At first glance, it may appear that Tocqueville is simply comparing the formalism of French Catholicism with the flourishing spirit of Puritanism in America. On a deeper level, however, I think that he is really praising the intensely personal religious nature that was generated from within and that, refined into its purest form, had become this country's defining spiritual tone.

All religions that leave a lasting mark on human beings and society must operate on both personal and institutional levels. All great religions are based on an absolute entity or truth and transcend differences of race, class, or social standing. They teach respect for the individual. However, as religious convictions evolve into religious movements, organizational demands emerge. In my view, these institutional aspects of religion must constantly adapt to the changing conditions of society. Furthermore, they should support and give primary consideration to the personal, individual aspects of belief. The unfortunate truth, however, is that few religious movements have been able to avoid the pitfall of organizational ossification. The development of a religion's institutional features ends up shackling and restraining the people whose interests it originally intended to serve. The external coercive powers of ecclesiastical institutions and associated ritual stifle the internal and spontaneous powers of faith, and the original purity of faith is lost. Because this is such a common occurrence, we tend to forget that it actually represents a reversal of the true function of religion.

Tocqueville considered it important that such abuses had been largely avoided by the Christian communities in America. He believed that the American people had preserved an essential purity of faith. This purity, and the degree to which religion was regarded as a matter of the inner life, is noted in remarks delivered by Ralph Waldo Emerson at Divinity College, Cambridge, in 1838. "That which shows God in me, fortifies me. That which shows God out of me, makes me a wart and a wen."[4]

In one viewpoint, the broad-minded, optimistic view of religion taken by Emerson and his contemporaries was only a momentary, happy respite in the spiritual affairs of modern times. Preceding it was an age of collusion between established religion and political authority; following it is an age of secularization that has reduced spiritual matters to private concern, stripped of any larger implications. It is not justified, however, to place this special period and its fruits completely in the past. The traditions of an inwardly-directed spirituality live on in the depths of the American historical experience and awareness.

Bushido and Self Control

If we turn to modern Japan, it is not easy to find there meaningful examples of this type of spirituality. After opening the country to the rest of the world in the mid-nineteenth century, Japan plunged headlong into the task of catching up with and overtaking the industrial nations of the West. The great Japanese author Soseki Natsume characterized that effort as an externally imposed process of civilization. He was right, in the sense that all of the goals and models for modernization came from outside. In their rush to catch up, the Japanese of that period did not feel that they had the time to work out the concepts associated with modernity for themselves.

Here, I would like to introduce an episode from the life of the Meiji-period educator and pioneer of Japanese-American friendship, Inazo Nitobe. Discussing religion with a Belgian acquaintance, Nitobe was asked whether the Japanese system provided for spiritual education. After careful consideration, Nitobe answered that, from the early seventeenth through the nineteenth centuries, it was *bushido*, or the way of the samurai, and not religion per se that had shaped the spiritual development of the Japanese people. In 1899

Nitobe published an English book entitled *Bushido: The Soul of Japan: An Exposition of Japanese Thought.*

There are a number of points in common between the spirituality of *bushido* and the philosophy of Protestantism and Puritanism. In part this accounts for the enthusiasm with which the writings of Benjamin Franklin were received in Meiji Japan. More important here, however, the spiritual development of the Japanese people, guided in part by the ideals of *bushido,* was largely inwardly directed. Inner motivation implies self-control; one acts in a correct and responsible manner not because one is forced to, but spontaneously and on one's own volition. During the Edo period, the incidence of crime and corruption was relatively low; this may be evidence of the concrete influence of an inwardly-directed spirituality on the workings of Japanese society. It is interesting to consider similar implications in Tocqueville's observation that, "In no country is criminal justice administered with more mildness than in the United States."[5]

Because the Japanese people of that period were motivated from within, they were able to attain a high degree of self-control and self-mastery. These qualities are among the best expressions of humanity, insofar as they help to create smoother social relations and less anxiety in personal contacts. Self-control and inner motivation as social ideals gave birth to a culture of distinctive beauty in Japan. It was noticed by many, among them Edward S. Morse, a graduate of Harvard and pioneer in archaeology in Japan. He wrote prolifically about the surprising beauty he found in the life and ways of ordinary Japanese. Walt Whitman was likewise struck by the air of dignity he sensed in the Japanese emissaries he saw walking the avenues of Manhattan.

With the growth of Japan's economic strength in recent years, contemporary Japanese-American relations, while still essentially friendly, have been strained by increasing disharmony. The stresses of the relationship were revealed at a deeper level in the Structural Impediments Initiative talks of 1990. Those discussions revealed frictions that were more cultural than economic. Cultures do not always respond amicably toward one another. Intercultural contacts that probe and question deeply-rooted, daily-life practices can provoke aversion or hostility. The need for restraint and self-control is never so necessary as when people are confronted with the confusion and tensions brought about by a collision of cultures. True partnership cannot be attained unless the effort to create it is based on mutual self-control at this inner, spiritual level.

The necessary inwardly generated self-control has been conspicuously lacking in modern Japan. Without it, Japan has tended to swing widely between extremes of overconfidence and timidity. Sometimes the nation has seemed unnecessarily obsequious in its relations with other countries, in particular with the West. Now we see an oddly resurgent arrogance based on nothing more than the most recent Gross National Product statistics. The approaching fiftieth anniversary of the Japanese attack on Pearl Harbor is a painful reminder of the enormous horror and destruction that the absence of self-control can cause.

Incidentally, Nitobe's *Bushido* played a very constructive role in the Portsmouth Conference at the end of the Russo-Japanese War in 1905. Soon after hostilities began, the Japanese government dispatched Kentaro Kaneko, a member of the House of Peers, to the United States to enlist the good offices of President Theodore Roosevelt in negotiating a settlement. Kaneko had been a classmate of Roosevelt at Harvard, and the two had maintained and strengthened their contacts in the intervening years. When the president requested a book that would explain the driving force behind the Japanese character and spiritual education in Japan, Kaneko gave him a copy of *Bushido*. A few months later, Roosevelt thanked Kaneko; the book, he said, had given him a clearer understanding of the Japanese character. Armed with this knowledge, he willingly took up the task of mediating the peace negotiations. In the far-from-peaceful history of modern Japanese-American relations, this episode is a refreshing example of mutual understanding.

The task that confronts us now is to revive the innate sources of human energy in a world marked by a deepening sense of spiritual desiccation. This task will not be an easy one, either for Japan or for the United States. Much depends on the attitudes we take. In that respect, the Buddhist doctrine of dependent origination, which shows how profoundly and inextricably our fates are interwoven, can make an important contribution.

Activating the Will to Harmony

One of the most important Buddhist concepts, dependent origination, holds that all beings and phenomena exist or occur in relation to other beings or phenomena. All things are linked in an intricate web of causation and connection, and nothing, whether in the realm of human affairs or natural phenomena, can exist or occur solely of its own accord. Greater emphasis is placed on the interdependent relationships between individuals than on the individual alone. However, as astute Western observers like Henri Bergson and Alfred North Whitehead have noted, overemphasis on interdependence can submerge the individual and reduce one's capacity for positive engagement in the world. Passivity, in fact, has been a pronounced historical tendency in Buddhist-influenced cultures. The deeper essence of Buddhism, however, goes beyond passivity to offer a level of interrelatedness that is uniquely dynamic, holistic, and generated from within.

We have noted that encounters between different cultures are not always amicable. The reality of opposing interests and even hostility must be acknowledged. What can be done to promote harmonious relationships? An episode from the life of Shakyamuni may help. Shakyamuni was once asked the following question: "We are told that life is precious. And yet all people live by killing and eating other living beings. Which living beings may we kill and which living beings must we not kill?" To this simple expression of doubt, Shakyamuni replied, "It is enough to kill the will to kill."

Shakyamuni's response is neither evasion nor deception, but is based on the concept of dependent origination. He is saying that, in seeking the kind of harmonious relationship expressed by respect for the sanctity of life, we must not limit ourselves to the phenomenal level where hostility and conflict (in this case, which living beings it is acceptable to kill and which not) undeniably exist. We must seek harmony on a deeper level—a level where it is truly possible to "kill the will to kill." More than objective awareness, we must achieve a state of compassion transcending distinctions between self and other. We need to feel the compassionate energy that beats within the depths of all people's subjective lives where the individual and the universal are merged. This is not the simplistic denial or abnegation of the individual self that Bergson and Whitehead criticize. It is the fusion of self and other. At the same time it is an expansion of the limited, ego-shackled self toward a greater self whose scale is as limitless and unbounded as the universe.

The teachings of Nichiren Buddhism include the passage: "Without life, environment cannot exist . . ." In other words, Buddhism regards life and its environment as two integral aspects of the same entity. The subjective world of the self and the objective world of its environment are not in opposition nor are they a duality. Instead, their relationship is characterized by inseparability and indivisibility. Neither is this unity a static one in which the two realms merge as they become objectified. The environment, which embraces all universal phenomena, cannot exist except in a dynamic relationship with the internally-generated activity of life itself. In practical terms, the most important question for us as individuals is how to activate the inner sources of energy and wisdom existing within our lives.

Let me illustrate this idea in relation to the previous discussion of conscience. I am sometimes asked to advise couples who are considering divorce. Divorce is a private matter whose final resolution rests with the two people involved. I encourage unhappy couples to remember that, from the Buddhist perspective, it is impossible to build personal happiness on the suffering of others. Such situations sometimes require painful reflection and forbearance. But through that pain one can strengthen and discipline the internal workings of the conscience—something Pascal understood very well. Ultimately, those concerned are able to minimize the destruction of human relationships that might otherwise result.

Our society today urgently needs the kind of inwardly directed spirituality to strengthen self-control and restraint. It is a quality that deepens our respect for the dignity of life. In a world where interpersonal relationships are becoming increasingly tenuous, greater self-control and discipline would also help restore and rejuvenate endangered feelings, including friendship, trust, and love, for without them there can be no rewarding and meaningful bonds between people.

It is my hope and my conviction that we will see a revival of philosophy in the broadest, Socratic meaning of the word. An age of soft power with its source in this kind of philosophy will bear true and rich fruit. In an age when national borders are breaking down, each of us will need the integrity of an internalized philosophy to qualify us for world citizenship. In that sense, those great standard-bearers of American thought, Emerson, Thoreau and Whitman, were all citizens of the world.

In closing, let me share with you this passage from Emerson's poem "Friendship," which was a particular favorite of mine in my youth.

> O friend, my bosom said,
> Through thee alone the sky is arched,
> Through thee the rose is red,
> All things through thee take nobler form
> And look beyond the earth,
> The millround of our fate appears
> A sunpath in thy worth.
> Me too thy nobleness has taught
> To master my despair;
> The fountains of my hidden life
> Are through thy friendship fair.[6]

NOTES

1. Blaise Pascal, *Provincial Letters (Les Provinciales),* Letter v, March 20, 1656, in Robert Maynard Hutchins, ed., *Pascal, Great Books of the Western World* (Chicago: Encyclopedia Britannica, Inc., 1952), 33:28.

2. Alexis de Tocqueville, *Democracy in America*(1835), trans. Henry Reeve (New York: Alfred A. Knopf, 1980), 1:309.

3. Ibid., 2:27.

4. Ralph Waldo Emerson, *The Complete Writings of Ralph Waldo Emerson* (WM. H. Wise & Co., 1930), 1:41.

5. Tocqueville, 2:166.

6. Emerson, 2:912.

The "weathermark" identifies this book as a production of Weatherhill, Inc., publishers of fine books on Asia and the Pacific. Editorial supervision: Jeff Hunter. Design supervision: Mariana Canelo. Cover design: D.S. Noble. Page composition: G&H Soho. Printing and binding: Quebecor, Kingsport. The typeface used is Bembo.